esq

A FISH
WILL RISE

A FISH
WILL RISE

D. Macer Wright

With illustrations by
VAL BIRO

DAVID & CHARLES
NEWTON ABBOT

FIRST PUBLISHED IN VOLUME FORM 1972
© 1972 BY D. MACER WRIGHT
ISBN 0 7153 5519 8

ACKNOWLEDGEMENT

Most of this book is based on my published
articles. For permission to reprint I
am indebted to the Editors of *Country Life*,
The Field, *Gamekeeper & Countryside*,
Shooting Times & Country Magazine, *Trout & Salmon*

D. M. W.

Printed in Great Britain by
Latimer Trend & Co Ltd Plymouth
for David & Charles (Holdings) Ltd, South Devon House
Newton Abbot, Devon

Contents

Foreword

FISHING BOOKS may teach or may beguile. This is not a teaching book and to say that it is a beguiling one would be to claim kinship with better men, for to beguile, so my dictionary tells me, is to divert attention from anything tedious or painful, and to do that a writer needs a goose quill or a nib of gold. We may assume that the first was used by the author of *The Compleat Angler*, and the second by the author of *Where The Bright Waters Meet*. I, alas, have had to make do with a ballpoint. However, if these reflections and recollections lighten an hour or two, that ubiquitous instrument will have served a not ignoble end.

D. MACER WRIGHT

Littledean,
Gloucestershire

CHAPTER 1

Along the River Bank

THE TITLE of this book is something of a borrowing, for it is
a hopeful assertion adapted from a note of melancholy resignation.

> We plunge and strive from spot to spot,
>   But not a fish will rise—
> In wonderment at our ill-luck,
>   Turn up our wistful eyes.

So wrote an aggrieved and anonymous versifier in the *Eclectic
Review* of July 1853. One's immediate reaction to this little
tale of woe must be that had the poetic angler plunged and
striven less, the fish might have risen more.

No doubt he strove valiantly enough, for one could scarcely
do otherwise with the man-killing rods our ancestors had to
use, but to plunge from spot to spot while flailing the air

with that brass-bound pole must have been the surest way ever devised of putting down all the fish within a hundred yards. Eyes, however wistful, turned however imploringly to heaven, would have seen no answering message of encouragement written on the skies.

I am reminded of a man I knew thirty years ago, who had spent his life making a large fortune and had finally retired to take up something for which, in his secret heart, he had always longed and which, in the manner of men beset by board meetings and balance sheets, he had visualised as the simple life. He bought a house in the chalk country, together with a trout stream, thus vindicating a lifetime in city pent, and making one grand gesture to save his soul.

Years of dining well but not too wisely, combined with that lack of exercise which tycoons today seek to make good by furious pedalling on stationary bicycles, had built around his bones a vast accumulation of flesh. By some incredible feat of physical contortion he would pull on his waders and lower himself into the river, always from the same spot where a convenient branch afforded a handhold. The right leg, which went in first, caused a definite shudder on the river bed. The left leg, entering at the moment when his hold on the tree was released, caused something akin to an earthquake.

When he waded forwards, there were bow waves a foot high round each leg. Like the troutless chap in the *Eclectic Review*, he plunged and strove from spot to spot, but never a fish did he rise. Then one day the inevitable happened. The branch broke, and twenty stone of fisherman lay in the water, rod, bag, net and all.

But he was a man with a sense of humour to match his Falstaffian proportions, and not afraid of a good story against himself. 'The plain truth is,' he admitted, 'I'm too damned fat for this fishing business.'

The moral is, if you want to be a fly fisherman, keep fit. A

man does not have to be small. Harry Plunket Greene was
6ft 4in and there have been few greater men to cast a fly upon
the waters. But I think the pre-eminent need is alertness.
To be alert to every tell-tale ripple on the water, every gentle
sip of a trout taking chironomid pupae, every tremble of a
trout on the feed, or as the fashionable have it, on the fin.
Alertness is the sixth sense. It is the sixth sense that makes the
fly fisher.

It is also a matter of temperament. I suppose the lure of
water is common to all anglers, from the boy absorbed in the
bright blob floating in some reedy old mere to the shark
fisher pitting brain and muscle against his gigantic quarry.
The fly fisher is usually a contemplative creature, sufficient
unto himself and preferring his own company, or at most
that of a congenial companion. Though fly fishers today are
really divided into two distinct species. We might call them
Homo sapiens solitudens and *Homo sapiens collectivens*. The latter
are those brave and brawny spirits of the Corporation Reservoir, long-hauling their forty-yard lines with a muscular
aplomb the very contemplation of which lays me prostrate
with fatigue. I possess neither their brawn, their bravery nor
their skill, still less their splendid addiction to collective bar-
gaining. To each his fish and his place for fishing.

The less we are able to grasp the moon, the more we value
it when we do take hold. Although my state of chronic
pauperism forbids any but the most modest chalk stream
fishing, there is nowhere in the whole universe of angling I
love and value more than the chalk streams, their water
meadows and willow trees. Heaven on earth is a wide and
tranquil valley, the skyline a spread of downland, the landscape a country of zig-zagging snipe and slow-flapping
herons, of purple loosestrife and marsh marigolds.

The country, let us say, of the Itchen valley, where the
sedges are eternally sighing and the *tuck-tuck-tuck* of the
warblers never ceases throughout the summer days. Where

the north wind sneaks along the river from somewhere over Beacon Hill, first a little breeze to temper the heat of June, then a series of laughing, malicious puffs just strong enough to blow the fly those few inches off course that will tell the two-pounder that something very odd is afoot—that glorious two-pounder whose deceiving demands the perfect throw, the highest finesse, with the fly creating no more disturbance than blown swansdown.

How I have cursed that mischief-making wind, and how valiantly have I striven not to curse it, to remain calm and collected, waiting to slip in between those puffs with what I hoped would be the deft flip of the Orange Quill to land it an inch above the trout's nose. That wind is the trout's ally. Nature calls to nature, elements warn the elemental, the wind breathes a mysterious note of caution to the fish. So the only way is to exploit the enemy's weakness, to wait until he pauses for breath, and then to cast my fly before he once more empties his lungs.

For second choice give me a brook that chortles over the rocks and stones of some Welsh fastness, where the dippers flit and the towering flanks of the hills know only wheatears and mountain sheep, and where the sky swallows the soaring buzzard.

Or else the trout pool, not too large, not too small, secret among ash and alder, smelling of wild garlic, haunt of silverhorns and pond olives and bickering coots.

But above all, the chalk stream, strong yet placid, wayward but never arrogant, bright with crowfoot, sombre with mare's-tail, where the sherry spinners fall at summer's dusk, the iron blues and the large dark olives brave the bitterest of the mad March winds. Whether the trout are rising or tailing or bulging, or simply shaking their sides with laughter at my feeble attempts to deceive, I will go to the Itchen, defying a hundred miles of maniac motorists, whenever the chance affords. Even if I catch nothing but weed scraps and flower heads and willow leaves, I shall have spent a few hours in Arcady, and my fortune will have been greater than that of kings and millionaires, who, I imagine, have little time to seek out that elusive land, and little peace to enjoy it if they do find it.

CHAPTER 2

My First Trout Stream

IN FLY fishing we advance from the dapping of oddments having an all-embracing anonymity to the casting of the daintiest characters which the skill and ingenuity of man can devise. It is fitting, therefore, that I should start from the banks of one of the sweetest little brooks that ever babbled beneath the skies of June where, more than forty years ago, I was initiated into something that would delight and dumbfound, bring despair and jubilation, and will continue thus until divine Providence shall say, 'Make this a good cast; it is your last.'

I shall always think of it as the most captivating stream into which any infant has slithered head-first while his father cast a fly. It was a day in June; the greendrake was up. At such a moment in his brief span, what fly fisher, though the fondest of parents, could be casting and baby-sitting at the same time?

The stream had been described thirty years before as 'a once troutful tributary'. Perhaps it was now less troutful, its trout smaller. But to me it teemed, and its inhabitants were leviathans. It rose in the greensand, headed north between sandhills and pine commons, then turned west with the great chalk ridge on its right. This it had for company all the way to the river, but the sandhills gave way to buttercup fields, woods and secret hollows, farmland and marshland and a hamlet among meadows, with only green paths to the outside world. And the world outside was more meadows and a farmhouse or two.

The brook chuckled and sparkled its way among crowfoot and under the willows of quiet villages unassailed by chain saws and scrambling bikes, villages that did not know their age-long peace was nearly ended.

The banks had meadow-sweet and campion, foxgloves, ragged robin, purple loosestrife. The copses were loud with black-caps and the wood warbler's explosive song. Wagtails flitted about the rippling water; the kingfisher sped on jewelled wing. On May nights, as far as a boy could see when the moon was full, this was a land of nightingales. Night sounds were the sounds of nature; all else was silence.

The stream had many turnings and cascades, and a deep, mysterious pool overhung by brooding pines, fringed by reedmace with fretful, sibilant leaves. It left the village and watercress beds, passed under a footbridge, crossed the common outside our house and flowed beneath another footbridge. The handrail of this was polished along its upper surface by many village hands, but the sides were grey with minutest lichens. The footwalk sagged in the middle. At first the crossing was a perilous adventure, but later one stood in the middle and rode up and down on the springy plank, watched by awe-struck small fry who were hoping it would break.

Along the valley road we bowled our hoops and spun our tops. The deadliest thing on four wheels was the doctor's sepulchral Humber; on two, it was the vicar's lady. And she, dear intrepid soul, with her 'machine' stacked fore and aft with comforts for the sick, the aged and the alcoholic, tended towards the suicidal rather than the homicidal. Yet by some fantastic feat of equilibrium she stayed a-wheel, and to see her slip smartly from the saddle and do a dozen paces at the double while hauling on the brakes was to see trick-cycling at its feminine best.

Opposite our house, on the brook's bank, was a tree that offered shade on hot summer days, and whose trunk gave cover from which to watch the spawning trout when fishing was done, for there they had a place in the loose gravel. Down stream was a mixed copse liberally supplied with caterpillars of hook-tips and mottled umbers which, from time to time, fell on the water, when all chance of their becoming moths came to an abrupt conclusion as there were always layabouts there who saw little reason to work for their living, when they could lie lazily in the cool water receiving titbits at leisure.

Here were the dapping stations, where I crouched away summer afternoons plying my father's strange and wonderful Palmers. I would creep on very catspaws through tangles of blackberries, nettles, and docks higher than myself, and then with as much composure as a seven-year-old could summon with his quarry lying in spotted glory beneath his feet, I would slide my rod through the herbage to lower the fly over the trout's nose.

He might field just above the surface, when he would flop back, and bang would go the gut until I had mastered the knack of giving him line in that split second between taking and flopping. When he took on the surface he was off like a bullet. Too much line, and he was straight into the snags; too little, and again, bang went the cast.

My father would choose what to me seemed the most impossible places, but always with the assurance that they held the best fish, and he was usually right, for he knew about such things, having in his time belaboured streams from Ludlow to Longparish. I still remember cracking my hand on an overhanging bough. The episode was painful, the fish was lost. My father, who held fast to the diabolical conviction that joy is born of tears, chalked it up as valuable experience. 'The wrist, the wrist,' he counselled, 'never the arm. You're striking a fish, not catching a ball.'

There were not many places where one could cast from the bank, so with graduation to a fly rod the delights of paddling tempered the disasters of casting. Paddling gave useful training. Nothing so breeds stealth in a young angler as walking barefoot over shingle and shifting silt. And few things are more disastrous than its first attempt in middle age.

How clearly I recall those formidable tunnels of alder and willow along which the fly had to go; those pools below banks enveloped in thistles from which, times without number, the fly had to be extricated at the penalty of pricked and bleeding fingers. With what despair one tried to reach those inviting deeps beneath the trailing willow boughs.

But it was not all fishing. We spent hours along the stream, fly nets in hand, catching specimens and misnaming them, or grovelling about the stream bed for what my father insisted on calling 'nymphae'. Over their names much argument ensued with our vicar who, fortified by a textbook fifty years old would peer through gold-rimmed pince-nez at my *Ecdyonurus dispar* and triumphantly pronounce it *Baëtis longicauda*. That kindly, God-loving man, innocent of guile except when fishing, was one of those whose Coachman, Grey Duster or Red Quill will bring trout after trout while the pedant is treated with derision. Such is the injustice of life. Or is the meek inheriting the earth?

As befitted a brook fisherman, the vicar turned Charles Cotton's 'first and principal rule for trout angling' of fine and far off, into fine and near to. Armed with a 6½ft wand, he would lay siege from a mere 15ft. In the casting of his line, the fly seldom more than 3in above the trout's nose, in the scarcely perceptible tightening of the strike, and in the finesse with which he brought to the net 12oz of supercharged *Salmo trutta*, was a rare and subtle artistry. I thought then, and I half think now, that the vicar, being a holy man, had received this gift from heaven, and my secret resolve was to become a parson.

Soon we moved to Essex. The valley of the blackcaps was a world away. From it school was farther away still, but fate was kind. The face of a certain master bore a haunting likeness to that of an aged trout that roamed my stream. For the beauty of his face I loved that master well.

CHAPTER 3

Fooled by a Caterpillar

THE PALMERS that danced upon that shade-dappled stream owed much to Alfred Ronalds, who was invariably known as Alfred the Great. They owed much, but not all, for my father had his own ideas, some of which might have caused Alfred's hackles to rise no less jauntily than those of his meticulous creations.

At the age of seven, one was both curious and trusting, avid to learn but uncritical, placing infinite faith in a father who knew all about 'nymphae'. So a furious battle of words was fought one day when my companion, perhaps an inch taller than myself, suddenly screeched, 'Caterpillars don't swim, you coot.'

He was absolutely right. Perhaps he is now sporting a Ph.D. for a thesis on the *Lepidoptera*. Sadly, but inevitably, faith gave way to doubt, and I found myself beginning to question the great Alfred and, what was worse, my infallible father.

My companion's remark, delivered on a note of piercing derision, was directed at the spectacle of myself not dapping a Large Red Palmer, but drawing it across the water. What caterpillar in its senses would cut such capers? It might lose its senses at finding itself cast upon the bosom of a stream, but it would hardly start swimming. Yet I was in company with Ronalds. 'The elastic fibres of the hackle open and close as it is drawn across the stream, and it displays its colours to the best advantage.'

What was this extraordinary object supposed to be, with locomotive powers unknown to any caterpillar, but which advertised its peculiar progress by flaunting its caterpillar colours? Ronalds is his usual splendidly unequivocal self. 'This is the caterpillar of *Arctia caja*, or the garden tiger moth.' No room for doubt there, and he recalls the exploits of a Thames angler who landed a trout of 3½lb, lost a larger one, took two more, one of 5½lb, and several others, all on the Large Red Palmer. The caterpillars that fell on my stream and were gratefully received by resident trout, were never those of the tiger moth. I recall only a few tiger moth caterpillars anywhere that were in imminent danger of ending up in a trout's gullet. But I am drawing not a Palmer but a red herring across the water, for the question is not whether trout take tiger moth or any other caterpillars, but whether an imitation drawn across the stream could possibly delude the fish into imagining that the object was a caterpillar. Ronalds took great pains over his Palmers. Instructions for the Large Red are sufficiently detailed to suggest that such details were important; 'black ostrich herl ribbed with gold twist and a red cock's hackle wrapped over it, with a good black feather near the head, shading off to a rich game red, and plenty of gold at the tail.'

It was a passable imitation of the fully grown caterpillar, and Ronalds seemed convinced that 'woolly bears' in general were of great attraction to trout. But why complicate matters by making them perform antics which no caterpillar has performed since caterpillars were made?

The explanation that, when drawn over the surface, they suggested struggling moths, will not do. I have never yet seen a moth skating across a stream; nothing is more alien to it than water. If one does fall on a river its wings are immediately made useless. In fact, it has great difficulty in lifting itself off perfectly still water, and usually fails. And in any case, caterpillars do not suddenly become moths, especially when they fall into water.

I have pondered this problem on and off ever since those

enraptured days and have been driven to the unsatisfactory conclusion that the scrupulous Ronalds stooped a little and was satisfied if his Palmers were all things to all fish. He does say that on a dropper a Palmer is probably taken for a beetle. My conclusion is a calumny that could hardly be more base, but if a caterpillar can be offered as a beetle, what other hideous rôle might it not be made to play?

It is said that palmer flies derived their name from the warriors returning from the Crusades, bearing branches of palm. They wandered far and wide, and woolly bear caterpillars also evince a wanderlust. But this does not, I fancy, include a propensity for crawling over water.

Perhaps it is one of those ancient puzzles of fly fishers that will remain to tease the firelit hours. After all, Palmers were among the first imitations devised in this country, contemporary with, and possibly pre-dating, Izaak Walton. Through whatever wild centuries roves back the palmer, to adapt Walter de la Mare, we shall probably never know its real mission in life.

CHAPTER 4

The Lie of the Trout

ALTHOUGH, in those far-off days of childhood, it was nearly ninety years since Ronalds had published *The Fly Fisher's Entomology*, this classic work could still serve as a valuable guide, not only to the identification of river bugs but also to the art of fly fishing in general. It can still do so, for it deals with things that are unchanging. Listen to almost any modern exponent of the art of catching trout, and you will hear echoes of Alfred Ronalds. Perhaps he echoed earlier men, but if so the sound was faint. He was a man who liked things at first-hand, and that meant from his own hand. As a 'population map', his section on *Haunts* can hardly be equalled, certainly not bettered. With its aid I read waters familiar and unfamiliar, as my father had done before me, and his father before him.

Reading the water is the ideal introduction to trout fishing, before ever a fly is cast. A trout is a perfect expression of nature's planned economy; housing, feeding, shelter, together with that degree of competition that ensures self-reliance and is the basis of all flourishing communities—a fact which, in human affairs, many people have yet to learn.

Ronalds was the true angler-observer. He set up a hide beside the Blythe, with three windows overlooking a 'scour' and whirlpools. He got someone to blast off with a gun to see if the row scared the fish; he and his friends, including the Rev Mr Brown of Grantwich, shouted 'in the loudest tones' at fish six feet away. To discover what trout like or dislike, he blew out ten dead houseflies through a tin tube, followed by thirty more treated with cayenne pepper and mustard.

Such experiments were not perhaps in the highest scientific class, but they taught Ronalds a lot of what he wanted to know, which was basically where trout lie and how they adapt themselves to stream flow, water depth, vegetation and so on.

I have often compared his pictorial abodes of trout with actual ones in streams I know tolerably well. The only large difference has been in the number of fish. There were far more then, which must be one reason why good catches were made in spite of the ham-fisted techniques forced on the angler by his Herculean tackle.

The places where trout lie should, says Ronalds, be carefully whipped. But before we start whipping, it is as well to select the spots. He tops his list with the head and tail of a rapid. Where the stream bends at the head of a swift glide, and where it tails off at the end, the flow lessens. At the head the water is gathering for the glide, at the tail the impetus is becoming spent. Food is carried at a reduced pace and is most easily snapped up in these stations.

Ronalds points out that his remarks are not strictly applicable to all streams, but says that perhaps they may not be found 'useless' for brooks and small rivers. Spot number two is the eddy formed by water passing round an obstruction in the current. This is a scaled-down version of the stream head, though the action on the water is different. It may be a miniature whirlpool where nymphs are caught up and spun round, or from which emerging duns find escape difficult, or a gentle lapping motion that impedes the carriage of spent spinners. The obstruction may be a boulder, a tree root, or as is only too frequent today, an old bedstead festooned with weeds.

Next come the scours, that is, pools and stretches of channel along the stream's edge where the current has scoured the banks and then resumed a straighter course, leaving cool deeps beneath the banks. These I always find among the most

The Lie of the Trout

productive places to whip. One of the best clues to a lie is Ronalds's 'Beggar's Balm', the froth that collects around tree roots. Dropped judiciously into this froth, my Herefordshire alder often has the desired effect. A current 'between weeds, where the bottom is gravel, is a sure harbour for fish'. True, and not only where the bottom is gravel. One trout channel I know runs between battalions of bulrushes. Getting the trout between these is a hazardous business.

Ronalds seems to have had a passion for italics, so it is not always quite clear whether he is emphasising a point's importance, or whether he entertains doubts as to the level of the reader's comprehension. Perhaps the latter, for he assures us that, under three or four ounces, trout are *too small* for the creel. Likewise in May and June, when the fish are strong, they are chiefly to be found 'in the more *rapid* parts of the water, and *on the feed* consequently'.

But, italics and possible non-comprehension apart, the point is well made. Large, strong fish do lie out near midstream, though often below the main current, and therefore frequently unseen in thickish water, when they are far more likely to be feeding below than taking surface food. In clear water they can be seen taking, as Ronalds says, 'with the greatest velocity', as they must in mid-stream.

There is a brook in a Welsh valley, one of many similar brooks, where those who do not trouble to read the water can waste much time on stretches where there are seldom any trout. Along these the water runs swiftly over shaley deposits worn to pebble size. The trout, though strong in proportion to their size, will not frequent such runs; the water is too swift, and too shallow to provide deeper shelter. Then you come to rocks and large boulders beneath which are deepish pools, and lesser rocks that create small waterfalls. Here trout lie as the breed must have lain since it first entered the stream, and nobody knows when that was. Here they take *Ecdyonurus torrentis*.

This water is very different from the Blythe, having fewer scours, since its margins are largely rock, and there are practically no weeds, yet it has its own version of stream heads and tails. Despite the comparative shallowness of the water and its extreme clarity, trout are all but invisible, partly because they are small and wonderfully camouflaged, and partly by virtue of their powers of concealment. Though I have fished this stream many times I never cease to marvel at the way in which a fly, flicked into seemingly fishless deeps below a stone, will be taken the moment it hits the surface.

Such places may teem with trout, but they may be separated by many yards of swift water that is virtually fishless. The casual fisherman coming to these haunts after flailing away to no purpose along the glides, might never realise that they held trout, and in any case he could easily fail to realise that if these places are empty it is because he has not appreciated the extreme wariness of wild fish.

When the stream is swift and the banks soft, with scours on the bends or beneath bank-side trees, the picture is rather different. In the scours we find the best of the trout, strong, relatively large, and well able to dart from cover into the current, snap their food and return. Here, the right fly dropped a foot or two above the scour, just on the edge of the current, will usually be taken.

Remote, unstocked waters cannot be expected to yield trout comparable in size to those from stocked hotel waters, but if one arrives on the latter during a dry-fly-only period, or if it is dry-fly-only at all times, and the fish have decided to feed underwater throughout the angler's stay, the effort of carrying back his basket will not be great. On my secluded streams one fishes according to the trout's choice.

Where the choice is wide the marrow scoop is invaluable. Ronalds was an enthusiast for examining the stomach contents of trout for the purpose of fly selection, and was severe on 'quacks and bunglers, who, inventing or espousing a new theory, whereby to hide their want of skill or spare their pains, would kill all fish with one fly as some doctors would cure all diseases with one pill'. One should note the difference between the rejected '*brown* hive bee' and the greedily swallowed 'March-*brown* fly'.

His illustration calls to mind all good sketch maps; those that once adorned detective novels, that embellish the pages of Pooh, or direct the reader to the regions wherein dwell Toad and his bright company. There is no Wild Wood, but in the tiniest print, almost indecipherable except through a glass, Ronalds points the way to Mappleton. Does it exist, or is it a place in some never-never land?

CHAPTER 5

In Search of the Black Gnat

IT HAS to be admitted—and for a disciple of Ronalds the admission is hard—that *The Fly Fisher's Entomology* seems to be guilty of at least one error in identification. I do not know whether Ronalds's apparent confusion between black gnats and reed smuts can be seen as the beginning of a confusion between the two that has existed almost until the present day. Note my qualifying phraseology, 'seems to be guilty' and 'apparent confusion'. I still cannot convince myself of a definite failure to distinguish black gnat from reed smut, and yet. . . .

The black gnat, says Ronalds, 'skims the brook all day long in immense crowds, flying at a great speed for about ten yards up and down the stream'. Does it, now? With deepest respect to Ronalds, and in a spirit of due humility, I suggest it does nothing of the kind. Does it not rather play over the water in swarms in a manner that to us poor mortals seems haphazard, even frenzied and positively futile? It dashes here, it dashes there, back and forth, seemingly looking for its wits. No doubt its erratic performance is really activated by urges beyond our comprehension, and is part of some highly developed pattern of behaviour which we do not understand. If it was as pointless as it seems there would be innumerable collisions but, like scurrying ants, swarming black gnats do not collide, or at least not very often.

Another thing they do not do is to fly 'at great speed up and down the stream'. The creature that does that is the reed smut.

We cannot doubt that Ronalds's Black Gnat representation

was effective, for he was not the man to offer anglers an un-proved fly and, of course, it is quite possible that trout took it when feeding on black gnats, but if it was offered when they were feeding on those species that were skimming up and down the brook, it seems likely that it was taken for an emerging reed smut or a spent female, or possibly an egg-laying form.

Confusion becomes confounded as we advance through piscatorial history to arrive at Leonard West. His black gnat was numbered among other gnats all having 'a true aquatic history', which 'may be seen emerging from the larval form on the surface of the water, when they either take flight or quietly drift ashore or downstream'.

He includes them under *Chironomidae*, and his illustration of the male is very lifelike. But again, it is not the black gnat, as it could not have been if it had an aquatic history. It is, as he claims, a chironomid species, though which one is not stated, and it is shown together with the commonest of the angler's recognised forms, ie *C. viridis* (green) and *C. tentans* (olive) which he calls green and olive gnats. We now arrive at confusion confounded and glorious; the black gnat of Ronalds was different from that of West, and neither seems to have been this insect.

Under the family name of *Tipulidae* and the generic name of *Chironomus*, Ronalds gives his golden dun midge. The illustration of this, showing a distinctly humped thorax and plumed antennae, leaves little doubt that it is a male chirono-mid, even though the wings and mating claspers are absent. So we arrive at the suspicion that although Ronalds dis-tinguished black gnats from chironomids, he mixed up the former with reed smuts, *Simulium*, while West did not dis-tinguish the first of these from the second. Ronalds's apparent failure in identification is made more real by his etching of the black gnat; this is more suggestive of a reed smut. His placing of chironomids in *Tipulidae* would not accord with present classification, under which this family name is given to the crane-flies.

When we come to J. W. Dunne we reach a stage of enlightenment. I do not know whether Halford was the first to point out that the body of the true female black gnat is not black, but as Dunne says, the 'joke' was rather spoiled by Halford's instructions that the copy of the female should have a jet-black body. 'As a matter of fact,' states Dunne, 'the body is a very dark olive,' and he gives his own dressing which produced 'an absolutely perfect imitation of colour and sheen'.

If we consult Skues we find that the species under his heading 'The Gnats' (*Silk, Fur and Feather*) are water-bred members of *Culicidae*, which is more strictly the mosquito family, so it is evident that he, too, was not dealing with the true black gnat. Later on, however, he does mention the black gnat in terms that make it pretty certain he is referring to the true species, but his dressing is a general gnat pattern.

Finally we come to Courtney Williams, who gives chapter and verse for the true species, *Bibio johannis*. On our journey we have doubtless left out other people whose thoughts and opinions might have helped to clarify or might have still further confused the issue, but we have seen enough to suggest that for many years the black gnat has travelled incognito, and that its habits have been confused with those of other species. In the minds of some anglers this insect still possesses a misty personality.

To lump chironomids, reed smuts and black gnats together under the embracing title of 'black gnats' or even more vaguely of 'gnats', might be justified by convenience if all these followed the same habits, but, of course, they do not. The fisherman who tries to separate the species, and to use the correct imitation in the correct manner is not being ultra-finicky, nor is he adopting a superior attitude. If, for example, coupled black gnats are on my pool and are obviously being taken, I am given a fair indication that what is needed is a Knotted Midge, and that if I thrash away with a sunk fly I shall probably thrash in vain.

It is, of course, true that trout will take a wet fly, sometimes quite deeply sunk, when black gnats are being absorbed, one of the best patterns in these circumstances being a Williams Favourite. But as they will also, in my experience, take several other sunk patterns fished nymph fashion, I wonder whether the Williams or the others have any connection at these times with the Black Gnat. Perhaps it is simply that trout are not feeding exclusively on this but are in the mood to take anything that looks takeable. To me, the catching of trout on sunk flies when the fish are obvious feeding on *B. johannis* is a somewhat hollow victory, though I suppose any victory is better than defeat if the only object is to catch one's limit.

As a dry fly for trout pools, the Black Gnat is of little value, as far as I can judge, when the naturals are on the water in masses, as they often are in humid or sweltering weather, for the artificial is then completely lost. But when numbers are lighter, particularly in August or early September, the dry pattern can be extremely effective. Identification of the species considered here is especially important for the pool fisher where chironomids are concerned. To fish a Black Gnat in any of its several imitations when trout are busy with chironomid pupae is usually a most unprofitable business. Yet it is often done, presumably because the angler mistakes flying chironomids for black gnats, though the habits and life histories of the two are completely different.

The need to distinguish between reed smuts and black gnats is evidently not so marked, purely from the point of view of catching fish, but to the fly-minded fisherman the greatest satisfaction comes not from chance imitation but from catching trout with a good representation of the fly being taken. However, since Halford recommended his own pattern for both reed smuts and black gnats, perhaps to differentiate between these is indeed to strain at a gnat.

Many water-bred 'gnats' and 'midges' have an extremely interesting biology. This is especially true of *Simulium* species, whose methods of feeding and self-preservation in larval form are examples of nature's inexhaustible ingenuity. It always strikes me as a matter for regret that many of the wonders of water life remain unregarded by fishermen throughout their angling days. Fishing, at its best, is not only catching fish.

CHAPTER 6

Rising the Non-Risers

ALFRED THE GREAT II has probably been invoked, either consciously or unconsciously, many times in the improvement of trout streams. I have certainly invoked him myself, and freely acknowledge his posthumous assistance. For he not only tells us where trout may be expected to lie in any satisfactory stream, but also implies where we may expect to encourage them to lie by improving an unsatisfactory one.

Unsatisfactory streams take various forms. I remember a stretch on the Cotswolds that was excellent trout water provided nobody wanted to fish. It carried some real whoppers, and plenty within the $\frac{3}{4}$–$1\frac{1}{2}$lb range, but as a dry-fly stream it gave no more encouragement than a bath tub. Admittedly, one could fish the nymph with success, but a limestone stream should be a paradise for the dry fly, the nymph being restricted to nymphing fish.

The trouble with it was that for most of this particular stretch it was too straight and too slow and gave trout little encouragement to rise. Non-rising trout are usually regarded as depressing creatures, but the determined dry-fly man accepts them as a challenge, presenting problems that he feels might be overcome by using a little imagination. Whether it is possible to persuade trout long settled to a diet of underwater food to mend their ways is rather doubtful, but it should be possible to attract new stock to the fly, before they, too, have sunk into bad habits.

For the sake of brevity let us regard streams as rising and non-rising. Any angler who has fished both moderately fast moving and lethargic waters would probably agree that the former could generally be termed rising, while many of the latter could not. Provided the fly is laid in the right place at the right moment and in the appropriate manner on a rising stream, it stands a chance of bringing up a trout, but on certain streams, or on certain of their stretches, dry flies will be ignored, or will be taken only by small fish.

Yet the non-rising water may be rich in weed, chock full of trout food and abundant in fly life. The marrow spoon used on such larger fish as we do catch, whether on nymph or, in extreme desperation, on worms, will tell a revealing tale. We resort to worms because of the imperative need to get fish out, to find what attracts them.

There may be among the extracted food various nymphs that we can or cannot recognise, but there will nearly always be snails or shrimps, or both, sometimes to the exclusion of all else. Here, then, lies a clue. The bigger fish, unlike the smaller ones which have not yet degenerated into gourmands, have long since gone to weed to stuff themselves on molluscan delights. And, of course, these mollusc-minded, uncatchable fish are the pride of the stream, pink-fleshed, halo spotted and eminently table-worthy.

The solution lies, I think, in speeding up the water, and

here we may refer again to the typical, well managed stream of moderate flow. Flow is the key word. The water is always perceptibly moving, often considerably faster than is immediately apparent, especially the chalk-stream. Flies on its surface are in regular transit. Many duns have difficulty in leaving the water. On emerging, they are carried some distance down; they rise, flutter, fall back on the water, to be carried still farther, and before they can make the final take-off they come to a fishy end. Spinners are completely at the mercy of the current. Feeding trout are at table; their meal is being brought to them on a plate. Thus they have every encouragement to partake of a varied diet and to come to the surface to enjoy it.

But what happens on the lethargic stream? The flow is too slow to carry flies down quickly enough to make it worth the trout's while to hang about waiting for them. Duns can get airborne more easily, for they are not flustered by eddies and whirlpools and sudden currents. Many never come within reach of trout, partly because they leave the water successfully, and partly because the lack of congenial lies on such water means there are few trout waiting anyway, except perhaps for those optimistic youngsters. Worldly trout will not take up station merely on the off-chance of snapping up a few scatty spinners.

It seems to me that dourness lies principally in the stream, not in the fish. Young trout are often willing to have a go on the surface, but they soon become discouraged and then join their elders among the snails and shrimps. There they stay, and all the dry flies in creation will not bring them up. What is needed is one of the various groin systems to deflect flow and create fast runnels that not only transport flies but eat into the opposite bank, gouging out holes that become pools. Into these, flies will be swept, and even if trout long resident in the water fail to turn up their noses at these newly established larders, new stock will soon appreciate their contents. Perhaps a few portly ones from below will, in time, come to realise that the water holds a succulence hitherto undreamed of. The simplest groin is a wood plank deep enough to stand somewhat above normal water level, long enough to make deflected water strike the opposite bank, though one can erect groins wherever they would create currents, irrespective of the effect on the opposite bank. Deeply driven stakes on each side hold them fast. Usually, two pools form, one in the hole in the opposite bank, and one in the lee of the groin. The outer edge of the groin should create small whirlpools or eddies, into which flies will be swept to the delight of trout waiting in pools. To ensure maximum impact on the opposite bank, water must be deflected from points just downstream of necks and bends, or from places where the stream narrows. Silting up behind the groins must be avoided, but if the angle is sufficient to guide water 'downstream and across', deposits should not be excessive. Groins should not be placed beneath bank-side trees, or where they would direct water beneath these; such placing could cause undermining of the roots. Long straight stretches are more difficult and take longer to transform, but groins, or cut-off dams sufficiently oblique and long enough to ensure that an adequate force of water is directed into the bank, should eventually create good pools.

A quarter mile, or thereabouts, length of water, hitherto dead for dry-fly fishing, could be made to contain a number of clearly-defined feeding grounds into which flies will be hurried on their way, and where trout will lie in wait for them. The nature of the intermediate stretches will not be, as it may seem, the same as before. Groins can influence these, creating changes of flow not easily discernible, but nonetheless valuable in giving the water new life. Such shifts of movement contribute much to trout water, the essence of which is variation. Often, groins and boulder dams can be temporary. These will be removed when they have done their job, or can be taken out for a time, while the results are watched. In any event, the original effects are not likely to be permanent, for no stream remains submissive to man's contrivance. But whatever the changes stemming from groin systems, they are usually beneficial.

In the type of stream dealt with here it is seldom necessary to buttress the banks behind gouged-out pools. This may well be needed where waters are subjected to strong spates. In their case groins serve a rather different purpose. A shallow line of shingle often builds up behind the temporary boulder dam. After the dam's removal this serves a useful purpose in low water; the current is guided into the newly-formed pool, keeping this aerated, and ensuring that it remains a suitable refuge for trout.

CHAPTER 7
Unhappy Mixtures

WHEN NATURE fashions a stream for the benefit alike of the kings and commoners of the fish world, she must view with some disfavour our relentless attempts to make it an exclusive pleasure ground for royalty. That, presumably, is why she re-populates a trout stream with grayling, to the everlasting chagrin of the keeper. Water containing only trout is to some extent a vacuum, and thus to some extent abhorred.

Nature's philosophy is based on the mixed economy, and nature is infinitely wiser, in the long run if not in the short, than we who seek to manipulate and distort her methods for our own ends. Mono-culture, whether of fish or french beans, is the most unnatural of all man's systems of husbandry. Sooner or later it brings disasters. Artifice is justified, often essential, but it must be founded on natural dispensations and it must recognise certain fundamental laws.

Like our friends the politicos, I am pontificating, but at least there is a gleam, however fitful, of common sense emerging. There is also a case, though a sad one and possibly rarer than is often thought, for keeping the stream exclusive to trout. It arises where the presence of other fish adds to an existing and perhaps severe condition of competition that is caused by the nature of the water. Such water is not, of course, ideal for trout; it is far from it, but it often has to be used by fly-fishing clubs in regions where ideal water does not exist.

In some respects, the multi-species philosophy may be applied to trout streams where these are variable in flow and pass over different geological formations. In certain circum-stances a stream may support a mixture of fish, including trout, without too much detriment to the latter, but my experience leads me to believe that where other fish do occur, trout will thrive only where conditions for their growth are sufficiently favourable to offset competition.

One stream I fish rises in the Severn watershed. It is liable to spates, sometimes quite violent, when the water becomes a churning torrent perhaps four feet above normal. In seasons of moderate rainfall it is excellent for trout, and almost as clear as a chalk stream, but during prolonged periods of rain, or after even short spells of heavy downpours, its tranquillity becomes seriously disturbed, resulting in a watery turmoil which trout must find distinctly uncomfortable.

The stream is a picture-book pattern of tumbling rapids, long slow stretches, loops, and pools almost the size of small ponds. This variety not only lends great charm and interest, but also provides haunts for fish species according to their natures. But as a trout stream it has definite snags, the end product of which is comparatively poor growth.

I am not one who is happy only when netting monster fish. My preference is for trout that respond to good waters, and make the best of what these offer. Certainly the occasional giant is a bonus which it would be foolish to reject, but for me trout fishing means catching specimens that have achieved the average weight of trout that feed well and make the grade through their own efforts, and not fish which have been blown up to the point of spontaneous combustion and then turned in.

It is disappointing to catch trout whose size shows that if they are making the best, it is simply the best of a bad job. Back they go, in the rather faint hope that if they elude others, they will wax fatter. In terms of length they may be takeable under the rules, but length is not all for those with memories, however dim, of hefty-shouldered, fat-bellied fish that once roamed our best streams. It is folly to sigh for the past. Those fat wild fish of one's boyhood were the last of a noble race, and during the intervening forty years or so the causes of the sorry decline have multiplied enormously.

This seems to me all the more reason for adopting a fairly stringent attitude when stock trout are introduced into the type of water where they are immediately at some disadvantage because of its general character.

The spate stream is very much of this type. Much weed growth is made unstable or even prevented from establishing itself; thus weed-borne trout food is in poor supply. Larvae and eggs of aquatic insects may be buried under transported mud; nymphs and minnows may be swept away. Where various fish species that also take trout food are present, competition for what remains of a depleted larder must further reduce the trouts' chances. In such circumstances good weight can hardly be expected.

Unfortunately, anglers whose experience is limited to this type of stream fishing do not always seem to realise that the trout they catch are inferior to those they might catch if conditions were different.

If trout are to be introduced into water that is not a true trout stream, but which has possibilities, then the very most should be made of those possibilities, and this may involve attention to considerably more than the one problem of competition. But to my mind the solution of this problem is fundamental to success.

Such water, if it varies appreciably in depth and flow, will probably contain roach and dace, possibly perch, and almost certainly pike, while grayling may also be present. Every trout fisher is aware of the danger of grayling, and of:

> The wary luce 'midst wreck and rushes hid,
> The scourge and terror of the scaly brood.

Pike are not so much competitors as assassins, while as competitors, grayling are in a class of their own.

Territorial definitions are fairly closely marked between

trout and roach, less so between trout and perch, and often non-existent between trout and dace. The last mentioned I see as perhaps the greatest robbers—apart from grayling— yet they are often tolerated to a degree which suggests that anglers do not fully appreciate the menace of this opportunist fish of catholic tastes. It is a beautiful little fish, bright-eyed, full of fun, and very palatable. I have loved it all my life, but not in trout streams of the type I am talking about.

Something like half its food consists of items from the trouts' larder; nymphs, chironomids, reed smuts and flies of many kinds. Perch and roach, though less likely to be within trout territory, nevertheless deplete trout food in some measure. Young perch takes nymphs, older ones minnows; perhaps a tenth of roach food constitutes such things as shrimps, immature stages of chironomids and reed smuts, and certain species not necessarily much represented by imitations, but nevertheless taken by trout.

So in spate streams, or for that matter in any stream that has features in some degree inimical to trout, and which carries coarse fish, conditions can be such that trout are doing little more than keeping afloat. The strongest and most belligerent will make fair weight, but there will often be many lanky specimens, and there can frequently be a surprisingly high number caught in September that have barely increased the weight at which they went in, since they have merely maintained the growth necessary to compensate for expenditure of energy. They have pedalled hard, but stayed in the same spot.

I am surprised at the resignation with which such fish are so often accepted as being normal to the stream. Surely they are normal only to sub-normal water. Elimination of coarse fish, and strict efforts to limit future populations, seem to me to be absolutely essential.

Limiting future populations means fishing rather than netting or resorting to electricity. Either or both of the latter methods may be needed when the stream is first taken over, but no matter how dedicated to the fly members may be, there must be some who are prepared to fish out the perch and dace and so on with rod and line. In any event, those whose dignity would be affronted at even the merest whisper of worms would find plenty of work for the fly, wet or dry.

CHAPTER 8

Mercies Large and Small

HILAIRE BELLOC called this land of Severn and Wye sodden and unkind. Perhaps he was suffering from jaundice. It has been my abode for fifteen years and I know it as rainy and kind. Do not its plains fatten the finest cattle in Christendom, its orchards make the purest perry, the rarest cider? And does not neighbouring Colne, the fairest of the fair, nurture trout to compare with the proudest of Test? Consider the names of our streams, from Shrewsbury town to Gloucester, from Hereford to Banbury: Arrow and Teme, Evenlode and Windrush, Marchfont Brook and Dickler, names that conjure swiftness, speak of wind and benediction and

> Such sights as youthful poets dream
> On summer eves by haunted stream.

Are they not names that befit a very Kingdom? Fie upon thy wicked slander, Master Belloc! Lovely indeed is thy South Country, but we of the Midlands have our glories too, our small mercies to be received with thanks, our large to be received with reverence.

We have a hundred streams for your delight, brothers of the fly rod, from the rocky, alder-fringed waters of mid-Wales, sometimes 10 or 20ft below banks that would give pause to a mountain goat, let alone a fisherman on the wrong side of fifty, to the pellucid ribbons of the Cotswolds and the comparatively little-known brooks of pastoral valleys.

Some of these valley brooks may carry surprisingly fat wild trout, and we do well to seek permission to try our fortune, either on permit in club water, where permits are available, or in splendid isolation among farmlands.

Throughout the length of many West Midland brooks, variation in flow, stream bed and vegetation, and the serpentine nature of the waters, combine to make fast glides, slow stretches and pools nearly large enough to qualify as ponds. All have fly life common to their kind; the mayfly, *Ephemera vulgata*, in the slower lengths, *E. danica* in the swifter, while along a stretch of perhaps 300 yards we pass the habitations of species needing such diverse conditions as the Iron Blue and the Pond Olive. A stroll past muddy haunts of mayfly nymphs brings us to shallow water rippling over rocks concealing shrimps and stone clingers.

For those of us who want to perfect our casting, who want not only to be skilled at orthodox methods but are keen to overcome all sorts of hazards by sleight of rod, there is nothing better than the tree-embowered farmland brooks, or drains as they are often unkindly called.

I once spent an afternoon backhand casting through a narrow gap between alders, watched from the opposite bank for long periods by a herd of apparently deeply interested Herefords. There were no fish there, or if there were to start with they must have wondered at the Pheasant-Tail Nymph that kept dropping from the heavens every few seconds, before they finally made off in disgust. The fishless exercise was well worth the energy expended, and with not a single fly lost, and the spots aimed for at last reached plumb on target, I counted the empty creel well worth its void.

In the Severn and Wye watersheds many streams like the one mentioned in the previous chapter are like liquid chocolate after heavy rain along the upper reaches, but the faster-flowing brooks flush out quite soon. These are generally very clear, with the stream bottom visible. They frequently shelve abruptly, from a few inches at the edges to perhaps 6ft in the middle, and the unwary wader can fill his boots in a second. And although there are many good gravelly stretches, there are also places where soft mud offers no footing, and one false step can sink a leg twelve inches.

One of my Gloucestershire streams has fine hatches of may-fly, but if the hatch comes off coloured water, swallows rather than trout account for the duns. We start with the March Brown, mainly in moderate numbers, for Gloucestershire streams are not truly March Brown water, and to find large hatches we have to go westwards to the Usk and other rivers of the Welsh border. This is followed by the large dark olive, *Baëtis rhodani*, for which a Blue Upright answers well. Then comes the medium olive, *B. tenax*, with, if we are lucky, a few *B. vernus*, though these are rarely abundant. Again, the Blue Upright fits the bill.

June sees us into the season of olives, iron blues and pale wateries, though of the latter, *B. bioculatus*, which, I think, is the only pale watery truly so called, is often lost then among the mayflies. Willow flies are common; also the Yellow Sally and many other stone-flies.

A list of all the species that occur and may be copied would read too much like a fly-dresser's catalogue, so as there is no bore like a fishing bore, let it suffice to say that on this stream, typical of so many moderately swift farmland waters with abundant cover and plenty of deepish pools, there is fly life for the dry-fly man and underwater food for those preferring nymph fishing, from March to September. And, with luck, there are trout to feed and be caught.

These waters seldom receive the attention that most chalk-stream men would consider indispensable, and there is no doubt that great improvements could be effected in such matters as weed planting to regulate flow and clear out silt, and clearing of the worst bank congestion. But nature is wonderfully adaptable, and what to a chalk-bred fisherman may seem a hopeless tangle of trees and bankside growth often shelters fine trout that another man used to such a perilous environment will sooner or later bring to his net.

Excessive clearance of waterside trees and vegetation can be the modern curse of trout fishing. One pond I know, once heavily tree-fringed, had good trout lying under the banks and cruising around within distance of any competent caster. Then the banks were ruthlessly grubbed. One might now be casting over a swimming pool. The trout are seldom seen under the banks, but rise outside the reach of the frustrated anglers.

Our Midland drains are for those who like to stalk their fish, exercise the grey matter and wade as warily as though walking barefoot on shingle. It is hard work. Constant scrambling up steep, slippery, nettle-infested banks—itself a triumph of mind over mud, of resolution over gravity—and seeking mere toe-holds of precarious root or tufty grass, are not for anglers whose fly fishing must be leisurely.

Because they are so variable, these waters cannot really be called trout brooks, though the fast glides have all the nature of brooks. They are less rapid than the glides of mountain streams, and at their heads and tails and at bankside scours offer ideal trout lies. But everywhere they are brook-rod streams. My son, who seems to have been attended at birth by the shade of some old master of the fly rod, is one of the few people I have watched who can manipulate a 9ft rod on a farmland drain. I certainly cannot. Many anglers, using this length, will tie their cast into knots that would baffle an Houdini. In the end they resort to the worm or to dapping. Both are a form of fishing, but to mess about with worms on fly water is to spurn one of nature's supreme benedictions.

CHAPTER 9

Fast by a Brook

THE TROUT brook—is there any more ravishing water? Well, yes, there is the chalk stream. To this I cannot yield even the lightest-hearted of frolic brooks, save perhaps the one in which I received my involuntary baptism, and in whose drops I am forever laved. Perhaps it was the brook some wandering scholar walked beside long ago, and then wrote down *broc*, which means water breaking forth.

Now as I thread the rings of my rod by a woodland brook, more than half a lifetime away from that moment of parental aberration, I think for a moment of Colonel Hawker of Longparish who, on the evening of 16 April 1814, 'was ludicrously amused with throwing a fly on horseback, which answers as well as on foot'. Earlier that day he caught in less than 2½ hours twenty-four trout, average weight 1lb, 'and many weighed 1½lb, also a great many fair-sized ones which

I threw in'. So no doubt he considered himself entitled to a spot of rodeo work in the cool of the evening, a decision encouraged, perhaps by the aid of an excellent cellar. Given all the circumstances, we may justly allow the sportive colonel his slightly eccentric entertainment.

But had he chanced across my local brook, I doubt whether such tactics would have brought much amusement. Here the angler, even without his horse, is 10ft high and still growing. The nervy little trout are right under your nose, and they do not consider the human nose a subject for study. The old saying that if you can see a trout it can see you is true enough when applied to this brook. If they do see you they are off, with a speed that is second only to that with which they eject a fly, and that cannot be far short of supersonic. There is nothing like hunger to sharpen the wits and stretch the nerves of trout, and those in this brook seem, like children, to be permanently ravenous.

Our brook drops down from 500ft to follow a winding, stony course through brown forest soil and clay and over strata here and there of magnesian limestone. It seldom exceeds four yards across; being swift, it has hollowed out some good pools on bends where banks occur.

My chance occupies a fraction of time, and if it is missed more than about twice it will not readily come again. Once pricked, twice shy is perhaps slightly over-stating things, but twice pricked is nearly always twice shy, and in such narrow water alarm spreads like an electric current.

To approach these trout in the expectation of seeing the take, and thus to strike on sight, is to court failure. All one sees is a sudden splutter of water and a split-second flash. As often as not this denotes ejection. Even fish in pools take like lightning; the instinct is obviously bred in the bone and is shared by all fish, no matter where they may lie.

There appears to be a dearth of insect life but this is an illusion. Nature having decreed that a brook shall carry trout, provides sufficiently for the existence of their particular kind. Man with his innumerable poisons is the enemy, not hunger. So the stream provides our trout with at least the means of life, if not the means of living it up. That cousin of the March Brown, *Ecdyonurus torrentis*, the March Brown itself, several *Baëtis* olives, iron blues and occasionally the Yellow Upright comprise the main diet. There is little or no nonsense about taking duns or spinners to the exclusion of nymphs, or vice versa; whatever is going is accepted, thus we are not so much concerned with entomology as with the arts of catching trout in circumstances that demand woodcraft almost up to Red Indian standards, and a strike that is about 10 per cent luck and 90 per cent telepathy. It is nice to think, when landing trout, that these add up to skill, but if we adults would see ourselves as we really are, we should go brook fishing with a youngster, when our reflexes would seem funereal.

A brook rod is quite essential. I use a beautiful little 6½ft split-cane wand made by my son, with which I can fish all day and still lift an elbow at nightfall. It is matt-finished; bright varnish, which I dislike as a finish, would be hopeless in sunlight. Practically all the casting is a matter of flicking into pools, under tree boughs, waterfalls and so on, and much of it must be made from a crouching position, usually in confined space. These restrictions, plus the necessity for contact with the fly immediately it lands, rule out any rod longer than mine. Fine-gauge cast is necessary, and with it I use a level white line, though whether this really is any less visible to trout than a brown or green one I do not know. For short casting a level line is better than a tapered one; the latter just falls limply on the water because the short length needed will not spring the rod.

Disciples of the incomparable Skues will know, though others may not, that he was a strong advocate of the left bank. He called it the bank of vantage and put forth sound arguments in its favour. On our narrow brook these have particular force. It is fatal to wave a rod over the water, and unless one is adept at back-hand work or with the left hand, upstream casting from the right bank means either an overland cast—Skues's cross-country cast—or else casting round natural cover which is often more of an obstruction than anything else, and in any case seldom hides the action of the rod and line. Back-hand casting overcomes the problem of direction to some extent, but its action makes rather difficult the strike that is often needed the moment the fly touches the water.

But on the left bank one can make horizontal casts from a crouching position, while a bush or a tree hides the angler without cramping his style, unless of course it is immediately surrounded by other trees and bushes. In fact this is often the case, and one must frequently cast through a high, narrow gap, which further points to the need for a rod which will throw a very short line, from a sort of modified steeple cast.

A tight line at all times is a basic tenet on this brook; just a little too much slack, and the fish will be lost. Also, slack line impels rough striking in an effort to counteract the surplus. One does not play these small trout in the accepted sense because in such narrow confines the fuss would put all the others down. They are not subjected to the indignity of being turned into a pendulum, but are lifted out quickly and cleanly, and straight-way despatched.

In general, the characteristics of the fish in this brook apply to most brook trout. One often hears water described as either wet fly or dry fly. Whether there is such a distinction among streams and rivers, it is not often found in brooks, because the trout are glad to try almost anything once. But in terms of artificials, 'anything' means a reasonable copy of the insects which inhabit the brook, and correct size is of the first importance. Large, over-dressed flies are useless. Until one gets to know a brook, it is sometimes difficult to decide what to use, for there never seems to be any fly life at all. In these circumstances, a lightly hackled March Brown, Williams Favourite, Partridge and Orange, Snipe and Yellow are as good as anything to launch upon the waters of chance and tribulation.

On my brook there is seldom a distinct rise period. But there are places, especially the pools, into which flies drift with fair regularity. These are haunted by the few half-pounders that occur, and which will take a dry fly almost any time.

Not the least task on a stony brook is to avoid cast breakage on protruding rocks, while the problem of drag when casting to the opposite bank is ever present. But these are accepted perils in the delicate little art of brook fishing, an art which demands continuous, feather-light throwing, using a short line and never allowing the fly to drift out of control.

Heaven lies about all trout waters—though the litter that lies about some public fishing-grounds suggests that many people cannot recognise heaven when they see it. The landscape of the trout beck is nearly always hill, valley and moorland, often wild and secret, frequently wet and windy, offering exercise of mind and body and refreshment of spirit. Trout will tease a man from break of day till fall of night. Colonel Hawker of Longparish would surely have loved them.

CHAPTER 10

Skues of the Itchen

IF THE Test was Colonel Hawker's river, the Itchen belongs for the rest of angling time to Skues. When we have shuffled off this mortal coil, do our spirits sometimes leave their celestial habitation to haunt the places to which that coil bound our earthly bodies? If they do, then the spirit of George Edward Mackenzie Skues, High Master of the Itchen, must indeed hover about the banks of his most beloved stream.

He died in August 1949, only a few days before his ninety-first birthday. For fifty-six years he fished the Abbots Barton water between Kingsworthy and Winchester. He was pre-eminently an iconoclast, 'one opposed to image-worship; one who assails old cherished errors and superstitions'. (*Chambers's Modern English Dictionary*.)

The error he assailed was not particularly old, but already it was becoming cherished. Halford's doctrine of the dry fly as the one exclusive method of chalk-stream fishing was to be challenged by Skues with all the warm logic at his command.

Warm, because this great fly fisherman was among the warmest-hearted and least dogmatic of men. Indignation at the slow acceptance of his view on the effectiveness of nymph fishing, and of the rightness of its ethics, scarcely enters his voluminous writings until, at the beginning of his eighties, he published *Nymph Fishing for Chalk Stream Trout*, when he found that 'there seems to be a movement on foot to re-rivet on the chalk stream angler the fetters of dry-fly purism from which I thought commonsense and the experience of the last quarter of a century had shaken him finally free'. There was indignation, fully justified, at the peculiar contraptions that he often called monstrosities, which were being sold as nymphs but bore not the slightest resemblance to any nymph that ever existed.

A truth is easily obscured, even lost, by its misapplication. Thus although Skues propagated a gospel that he knew was right, his endeavours suffered at the hands of tackle dealers who produced these bizarre creations, and of fishermen who used them. Fished upstream they scared the wits out of trout unfortunate enough to encounter them; fished down they became mere lures, and Skues was in any case vehemently opposed to the down-stream wet fly on chalk streams.

We learn from C. F. Walker's biographical note to his collection of the *Angling Letters of G. E. M. Skues*, that his subject caught his first trout as a Winchester schoolboy of seventeen. This memorable event occurred with a sunk fly on the Old Barge section. There followed thirteen piscatorially undistinguished years until, in May 1883, he became the guest of Irwin Cox on the Abbots Barton stretch. So began an association between angler and water that lasted until 1938, when the angler was eighty, and which has now passed into legend. No fly fisherman can think of the Itchen without Skues, or of Skues without the Itchen.

In *Minor Tactics* he distinguishes between 'dead knowledge, which is reading or imitation, and live knowledge, which is experience'. Though he never gave less than generous praise to past masters, opining for example that Halford's *Dry Fly Fishing in Theory and Practice* was 'the greatest work which has ever seen the light on the subject of angling for trout and grayling', he was not, as his experience grew, content to rest on their wisdom.

He started off with the sole ambition 'to follow in the steps of the masters of chalk stream angling', to do what was laid down for him—that and no other, and he looked back 'with some shame at the slowness to take a hint from experience'.

The first hint came on a September day in 1892, with black gnats thick upon the water and trout smutting freely. He followed Halford to the letter; Pink Wickham, Silver Sedge, Red Quill, and rang all the changes. He started at 9.30 am, and by 3 pm his creel was still clean. Then came the revelation, though it was not recognised, being merely put by as an experience for use on the next September smutting day.

It came in the form of a shop-tied Dark Olive Quill dressed to float, but with a hen's hackle, which made it fairly useless as a floater (a pretty reflection on the fly dresser's knowledge). It was directed at a smutting trout; on the second cast it went under and was promptly taken, but in his excitement Skues struck too hard and left it behind.

He mounted another that again went under and was taken. This time he caught his fish, whose 'belly contained a solid ball of black gnats, and not a dun of any sort'. During the next hour or so he secured four brace more by exactly the same method.

On a September day two years later he had another hint, 'as pointed and definite as one could get from the hind leg of a mule', but again he did not take it. Droves of duns drifted in little fleets hugging the bank, where trout were in force, feeding steadily. Who indeed would have taken any but the classic hints of Halford—Quills of all shades, Gold Ribbed Hare's Ear, Ogden's Fancy, Wickham? With these he 'battered' the trout, only to leave them rising with un-diminished energy when he sat down for lunch.

After lunch, what should by now have been the revelation came with an old-fashioned Blue Dun, also dressed to float, but which soon sank. On the second cast it was taken, and so with the following three casts. 'Still I did not realise that I was on the edge of an adventure.'

Several years later Skues began seriously to consider the phenomenon of bulging trout, and effected 'some sort of solution with a variant of Greenwell's and Tup's Indis-pensable'. As time progressed, he gained vast experience, which gave rise to the historic statement, 'To cast a dry fly to a bulging trout is to cast without any reasonable hope of attracting the trout. I have done it many times, and I ought to know'.

He was a supreme exponent of the art of studying trout, their habits and haunts, their life and means of livelihood. He acquired an ability amounting almost to genius to detect from their rise patterns what trout were feeding on. If genius is an infinite capacity for taking pains, we may justly apply that overworked term to Skues.

Nymph fishing was never advanced to replace the dry fly, but as a supplementary measure when fish were taking nymphs. His entire philosophy was based upon the extreme absurdity of pitching dry flies at nymphing trout, and he has been vindicated *ad infinitum*. Skues was rarely a graphic writer, preferring tight lines to straying paragraphs, yet for those of us who shared with his latter heyday the heyday of boyhood, he evokes all the splendour of times when the world was a water meadow, and the most important thing in life was catching trout.

His writings contain countless facts of the greatest value. 'The checked fish goes to weed; the unchecked fish flounders on the surface.' These are worth the price of a season on the Test. 'Trout will not as a rule take a fly to which weed is attached.' Many an angler, too impatient to clear his fly of weed, could take this statement to heart and thereby catch more fish.

In his last book, surely his testament of faith, the final statement, omitting the last appendix-like pages, is splendidly, magisterially, to the point. 'Of course Halford was wrong in saying that the trout would not look at the artificial nymph. Not only I, but many others, have proved that over and over again.' The words close an era. It was Skues's era; he spanned it, perhaps created it. In the art of fly fishing little of moment has been discovered since. He will remain as Master for generations to come.

CHAPTER 11

The Fly and the Driver

SKUES DID not, we are told, suffer fools with any marked degree of enthusiasm. Nevertheless, it is clear from his published letters that his patience was almost inexhaustible when it came to genuine matters of fly fishing. He was irked by those 'monstrosities' for they were spurious objects, and only the genuine had any place in his scheme of things. So when he quotes the remark of George Selwyn Marryat, possibly the greatest fly dresser of all time, that 'it's not the fly, it's the driver', we can be certain he took it for granted that Marryat meant a correctly dressed fly.

As a pun, the remark may stand with any of the quips of Tom Hood or of Charles Lamb and his cronies, but as a fishing dictum it seems to me, in spite of its exalted source, to be a little shaky for this present age. Or perhaps I should put it the other way. The dictum remains sound, but the age has become shaky.

It was all very well for George Marryat; he was not only a wizard of the fly bench but also a marvel on the river. He could do things with a trout fly—any trout fly—that would make an ordinary performer look like a boy with a bent pin. Many of us, if we will but admit it, are ordinary performers, as far from Marryat as the family motorist is from the rally champion. For us of the legion, if not of the damned, then of the dogged, it is very much the fly. Not merely the one that is correctly chosen, but the one that is correctly dressed, and there's the rub.

Early in my fishing career I came to regard fishers of chalk streams as persons touched by divinity. In the course of more mature reflection this opinion became somewhat modified, but I have always believed that among trout fishermen who really know what they are doing, the chalk stream habitué reigns supreme. So it came as a shock to find a customer in a tackle dealer's, whose clients number many chalk-stream men, turning up his nose at a perfect Iron Blue on the grounds that it was 'a bit skimpy'.

In fact it was not skimpy at all; it was evidently a fly of good breeding, for it was well-dressed, but not over-dressed. The customer was placing an inflated value on the fuzzy-looking objects that are turned out in tens of thousands by some mass producers, presumably in the conviction that anglers expect their money's worth, and that value for money means a multiplicity of hackles. Also, of course, when half of them fall out during the first day's fishing there are still plenty left.

I do not want to denigrate all mass producers of trout flies. Some turn out very good samples, and it may be that my irrational but nevertheless ineradicable detestation of mass production blinds me to its many virtues. But in the matter of trout flies I cannot easily see how their being churned out on a factory basis can have much point of contact with the lively, delicate things they purport to represent.

The true fly-dresser is always a fisherman and he is often as active with binoculars and butterfly net as he is with his fishing rod. He watches duns emerging, sailing on the current, taking flight. He witnesses the mating dance, the falling of spinners and their carriage downstream. He comes to know how a dun sails along, wings a-cock, how a spent spinner's wings are flat, limp and useless, and he is adept at lending these various appearances to his artificials. He knows how many hackles will make his dun just kiss the water, and ensure that it will ride without being soaked in flotant, for a sticky-looking artificial is miles away from the freshness of a newly emerged natural.

The masters of the art, Halford, Skues, Marryat, and many who neither sought fame nor had it thrust upon them, were of this brotherhood (though they may not have had binoculars) as are their disciples today, and common to all is an abhorrence of the over-dressed fly. What some of the old-timers would have said about modern mass-produced mayflies can only be imagined; what one fly-dresser of my acquaintance says of them is best left out of print.

Mayflies are certainly large, but so many artificials are larger than life. Some are absolute horrors, calculated to drive any trout that is not half-witted into giving them a wide berth. If those who produce such things tried fishing them they would probably find that very often the most effective size is slightly smaller than the natural.

In the matter of 'spider-flies'—wet March Brown, Williams, and the general Snipe and Partridge series—it is remarkable, but nevertheless a fact that some people reject these in favour of fancy patterns for upstream nymphing. Some of these patterns do have a certain nymph-like appearance in running water, but certainly not the gaudier ones, and most definitely not large ones. Very few are as effective for upstream nymphing, or for nymphing in still waters, as are the spider patterns, or the true nymph types. They are not meant for nymph fishing, but because the correct patterns are drab little objects compared with the flashers, the latter are often preferred, perhaps because they seem to offer more for the money. What they do offer, if they are good ones, are passable representations of fish fry, but they offer scarcely any likeness to swimming nymphs, which are almost invariably drab-coloured, greenish-brown or brownish-green, and whose structure is not, and is not intended to be, suggested by the standard fancy patterns.

Mass-produced articles are necessarily standardised, which may be just the thing in this age of the great levellers, but between the many petty little affairs of our material world and the endless miracles of unconforming nature, there is a disparity which mass production cannot reconcile. This is very evident in the making of trout flies. Certain of the *Ephemeroptera* vary in colour and size according to region and time of year. The July dun, *Baëtis scambus*, of the Cotswold streams is often slightly darker than the same species from the south-west, a fact which J. R. Harris established. He also found that the blue-winged olives from the Kennet were larger and slightly brighter than specimens from Somerset, while many fly fishermen will know that the large dark olives of spring are larger than those appearing in autumn, and that the latter are usually lighter.

Unfortunately, even a natural fly of a more or less standard colour is not always well represented by mass production. To take our Iron Blue again, the body of the female spinner of *Baëtis pumilus* is predominantly reddish-brown, the abdomen being mahogany coloured from which the popular name Little Claret Spinner is derived, while the body of the male spinner is divided in colour between white, brown and olive. Halford has a first-rate pattern for the male, using for the body stripped condor dyed dark olive-green. There are several dressings for the female apart from standard patterns like the Houghton Ruby. Some have for the body dark claret seal's fur and claret silk for the female spinner, and mole's fur and claret silk for the dun; but whatever materials are used, the body is always dark. Yet I have in front of me a shop-bought specimen the body of which is bright sealing-wax red.

It may possibly hook a fish, but that is not the point. As a representation of the Iron Blue, it would evoke expletives from my friend of the mayflies that would ignite this paper.

CHAPTER 12

Epicures in Still Waters

STILL WATERS is not altogether appropriate because the trout pools I fish are fed by streams, but as these are small and the pools vary in size from about three acres to an acre, and are about 10ft deep in the middle, the visible effects of the currents are not great.

Those whose temperament inclines towards rocky rivers or chalk streams are not always at home on secluded pools. Yet in their environment and the methods they offer, these have an endless fascination. They possess an intimacy seldom found on large waters; a trout pool is 'a still point of the turning world'. Chiff-chaffs are in residence, coots sound their toy hooters, thrushes chuckle and splutter, seeming to applaud or deride one's efforts as they think fit, and squabbling moorhens, unlike squabbling humans, make a kind of music.

But the methods offered; I can hear the chalk-stream

pundits muttering that there are no methods, that pool fishing is just glorified spinning, without subtlety or touch. Not so, eminent sirs. We do not merely thrash about with flashers. During the season's initial feeding rampage we might hook a fish on a bit of old bootlace, but that phase is short-lived. Within a few days we are finding our depth and fishing seriously with patterns that copy the underwater life in which the ponds abound. This is a delicate business, demanding enormous concentration for the taking of such things as surface nymphs and chironomid pupae is often preceded by a gentle sucking, which is seen as no more than an almost imperceptible drawing away of the cast. Strike too soon and you whisk the hook out of the trout's open mouth.

On my pool chironomid pupae are among our best lures. In the emergence period, natural pupae ascend to the surface and hang from the film for a few minutes before breaking out as adults. Trout will take avidly. The main snag is that these species inhabit much deeper water, and if long casting is hindered by waterside trees, one often has to watch impotently many an excellent rise far out of reach.

Our springtime species are primarily the small black midges. We see less of the larger summer types like the olive and green midge, *Chironomus tentans* and *C. viridis*, the swift, surface-flying adults of which are the Blagdon Buzzers. Fishing these pupae is a matter of casting, waiting for a minute or two, with an occasional twitch, and casting again. The cast is greased almost up to the point, so that the pupa hangs realistically. Compared to fishing a dry fly on a stream, this method is virtually static. There is little or no movement in calm weather, but when the pupa does drift towards the angler, line adjustment to maintain contact is essential. This manipulation of the line must be done with extreme care, for under gently drifting conditions the water surface is scarcely ruffled, and rough line pulling is clearly discernible to fish cruising near the surface.

Another imitation that can be successful, though response to it is variable, is the Lesser Water Boatman, for which we have a general pattern to copy in many of the *Corixidae*. These make trips to the surface, swimming strongly, and we work the patterns in quick jerks with variations in the timing, using an ungreased cast.

Because of the difficulty in imitating much pond life we must make do with a certain amount of nondescripts, though C. F. Walker's excellent underwater patterns have substantially enlarged the range of imitations. The greatest difficulty, once the fish becomes perceptive, is to know how to work such things as spider patters, Williams Favourite, Partridge and Orange, lightly dressed March Browns and so on. The days when our trout will grab at a Silver and Blue Teal or a Butcher twinkling through the water are almost a memory by mid-May, and one quickly becomes disabused of any idea that such things will catch fish. Particularly with a floating line, using these is about as profitable as fishing the average water-butt, though in muddy floodwater flashers fished deep on a sinking line are a good proposition.

I am no purist but I confess to a sense of irritation if a trout takes a spider fly fished nymph fashion and again on the same fly fished fast, especially if the pattern represents a non-indigenous species. My wife, who does not fish but is rich in feminine logic, asks whether it matters a hoot what the trout took the beastly thing for, so long as it took it. In the matter of true nymph patterns, if such they may be called, one is approaching more to reality, even though imitation is general within the class one is trying to copy, rather than specific. It is interesting to compare the results of working fast a fly which can be taken as a nymph if worked nymph fashion, with those of working a true nymph fast. By fast I mean in the manner of a flasher. The first type will take fish with both methods; the second hardly ever when simply drawn fast through the water. This suggests to me that trout are wary of anything which, though it may be a first-rate imitation of a nymph, is not being worked in a manner that simulates a nymph's movements.

But I do not agree with the idea that artificial nymphs should necessarily be 'un-worked' in still waters. It all depends on the types indigenous to one's water. For example, nymphs of the genus *Siphlonurus* both dart and swim very rapidly, particularly along the margins of weed beds; the *Cloëon* nymphs of ponds—the lake and pond olives—are extremely fast swimmers, while those of the claret dun, *Leptophlebia vespertina*, are comparatively sluggish. Perhaps the biggest obstacle to giving life to imitations of sluggish nymphs on pond bottoms is the impossibility of simulating their tracheal gill movements. The term sluggish can be related only to the relatively stationary position in the water; the nymph is in fact quivering in order to breathe, and an artificial lying inert on the mud must present a most un-nymphlike spectacle to fish. The gills can be represented to some extent in the dressing, but they cannot be given life. It is only when a nymph is at the surface immediately before the emergence of the dun that it can be considered motion-less, and even then there are moments of agitation during emergence.

Thus the pond angler has a wider scope even within the nymph range than is often supposed. He can fish on the bottom with some hope of success, and in the middle and surface regions with good hope. If his pond carries a variety species he can explore open water, weed-bed margins, and weed-bed channels if lake olives are about, though this is obviously fraught with some peril.

There does seem to be an essential difference in the fast working of nymphs and flashers. If the trout take the latter to be fish fry, they appear to do so mainly early in the season when their discrimination is undeveloped and their need for food such that they will grab at anything that looks edible. I have always doubted whether the conventional method of working flashers simulates lifelike motions in still water, where there is no current to aid movement. We cannot greatly vary the line of travel when retrieving line in the way normal to this type of fishing.

When simulating swimming nymphs a different technique is needed. The rod tip must be twitched occasionally, vertically and laterally; line retrieve must be erratic, jerky, never rough. All in water that is often glassy calm, rarely much disturbed. Heresy though it may sound, I believe that more skill is demanded in fishing nymphs in ponds than in streams (except in the slower reaches of chalk streams, where the demands are not dissimilar). In swift water, the stream fisherman must be deft at keeping contact with his nymph as it hurtles downstream, but the greater the turbulence the more are deficiencies in technique and fly pattern covered up. Fish have no time to ponder; they must grab to live.

A pond, on the contrary, is ideal for pondering. Fish can watch every badly-thrown cast writhing above; they are sensitive to the plop of every over-weighted or carelessly cast artificial. The noise of a line ripped off fast water is lost; on a pond it is as good as saying, 'Look out, here I come'. And any illusion that trout will take whatever nymph pattern you offer is soon dispelled by the spectacle of their complete indifference to a surface pattern that does not represent an inhabitant of the pond.

We come back to the old question of how choosy trout can afford to be, and we see that while there is scarcely any point of similarity between the fast, rocky stream and the rich pool, there is a distinct similarity between the pool and the chalk-stream. In both these trout can often take it or leave it, as the fancy moves them. In the rich pond they frequently have an even greater choice than in the chalk stream; if chironomid pupae or pond olive nymphs are on the menu, and if these are what they want, then it is exceed-

ingly difficult to tempt them with anything else, except
during the early part of the season, and possibly again at the
end, more especially where rainbows are concerned.

There was a good illustration of reaction to food in my
pools a few years ago when we netted out some five hundred
brook trout from a nearby stream that was to be used for
salmon experiments, and put them into the pools. Their
immediate response was to grab at almost any type of small
fly, just as they had done in the brook. But after a time, when
they had discovered that the pools provided food and security
such as they had never known before, their feeding habits
became similar to those of the ordinary pool trout, and they
then proved to be just as hard to please as their epicurean
brethren.

CHAPTER 13

Persuasion with the Wet Fly

'THE FETTERS of dry-fly purism' which Skues sought to break still encumber the minds of some trout fishermen. For such men I cannot avoid a certain respect and affection. Their approach may be illogical, hidebound, years out of date, yet underlying it are things all too rare these days, a sense of fair play, a devotion to what they conceive to be right and a determination not to lower what they regard as proper standards.

I think they are wrong if they look upon nymph fishing as unfair, and very wrong indeed if they imagine that it takes too many fish, for skilled nymph anglers are not all that common, and unskilled ones will not appreciably reduce the stock of trout. Nevertheless, the sense of fair play, even though misconceived, denies nobody but the purists themselves, and if they are willing to forfeit the chances of taking trout on anything but dry flies, they demonstrate active service (or should it be passive?) to an ideal, instead of the mere lip-service which so many people pay to ideals, no matter how loudly they thunder these in the market places.

The dry-fly purist is perpetuating what he sees as a good tradition; he is upholding a code of ethics handed down from an age that valued such things. He is therefore not only rare among modern fishermen, but what is more important, rare among all men in these days when the very idea of ethics is a subject for laughter.

My friend Charles, though a dedicated dry-fly man, is not now above using the wet fly on waters outside his sacred chalk stream, after his visit to my pool, though his own beat will never be tickled by him with any but the hackles of a floater.

For this first visit, not reasoned argument but low cunning was needed. Charles is a true Halfordian; if his trip to the pool was to be rewarded with the visitor's limit some measure of subterfuge was essential. I salved a slightly uneasy conscience by telling myself that it was cunning in a good cause. Few phrases have been so twisted to make expediency seem a righteous act, or to justify ignoble deeds, as that of Matthew Prior, who did not say: 'The end justifies the means,' but who said 'The end must justify the means.' In this particular case I felt that due respect would be paid to Prior's dictum, and I was secure in the belief that my friend, who is a scholar of Horace, would see in my descent to the unmentionable some touch of the *splendide mendax*.

The occasion was rendered a shade unpropitious by the fact that he was still fuming after having read an advertisement for a 'fish attractor' in the form of some odious stuff which, squirted on the fly, brought up the fish. I tried to soothe his outraged feelings by reminding him that this was nothing new, and that it would doubtless pass as it has passed before. In Sir Humphrey Davy's time, anglers used scented worms. And in 1807, a lecturer assured his audience that trout were attracted by 'the emanations of odorate bodies'. We agreed that whichever way one interpreted this, it sounded quite disgusting, and on that note I was glad to record mentally that we were one.

We arrived at the pool during those delicious twenty minutes or so before the evening rise. My friend is nearly exclusively a chalk-stream man. This was his first visit to the pool and he wished to place himself 'entirely in my hands', subject only to the proviso that he wanted to fish the dry fly, and it went without saying that he wanted to fish the rise. So he should. Nothing could have been better for my fell purpose.

Congregations of black gnats began playing over the water; not too many to smother an artificial, not too few to pass unnoticed. 'Horrible objects', muttered Charles, as I handed him a Knotted Midge. While he was tying this on, I made a casual cast into a deep bay with a Dunkeld. At once I realised that this was a social blunder; a nymph my friend might just have tolerated, but such an unspeakable thing as a Dunkeld had never yet sullied his water.

Well, this handsome creation of jungle cock feathers had sullied mine, and this time to good effect, for suddenly there was a thump that travelled down to the rod butt and a flashing, silvery rainbow leapt clear of the water. Down went the rod just in time to save the cast from that lashing tail. My rainbow was a skilled tactician. After some ferocious plunging on the surface, he disappeared from sight. The line veered to my right and I knew the fish was making for the tangled growth beneath an alder where he would snap the cast as easily as one snaps modern cotton. Vertical strain was useless. That might slow him, but it would not stop him. Side strain, with the rod parallel to the water and firm but gentle pressure to my left, was the only way. This turned him, and finally he came to the net.

My friend's expression was aloof. The rise had now started, and he went off with his midge to select a rising fish. Now I knew, but he did not know, that the early part of our evening rise is usually different from the later part. It is also quite different from that of his chalk stream. The trout were making a fine old hullabaloo, visibly breaking surface and often jumping a foot or more clear. Methodically, and with exquisite precision, my friend laid his fly dead in the centre of ring after ring.

My strategy was to time things to the nicety which was necessary if he was to catch fish on both wet and dry fly. I was pretty certain that he would succeed later with a dry pattern, and I was equally sure that he stood a good chance at this present time with a nymph, but virtually none with his marvellously-presented floaters.

The time had come to let him into the awful secret that those acrobatic fish were not in the least interested in flies, but were chasing rapidly darting nymphs. Such pursuit results again and again in the vigorous surface breaking that was continuing with unabated energy.

'It's no use, Charles,' I said. 'You will have to sink your prejudices in the form of a nymph.' Reluctantly, but with evident curiosity, he agreed to this breaching of his principles. After all, this was not a chalk stream, and a nymph could not —by any trick of the fly dresser's art—be compared with that 'preposterous' Dunkeld. In fact, so abandoned had he suddenly become that his hand hovered tentatively over a Connemara Black, until I told him that it was almost useless on this pool.

On went a Pond Olive nymph, and Charles, who is of that happy breed who can master new departures in fishing after the briefest introduction, was soon playing it just below the surface with a dexterity that made me wonder why I had taken so long to learn. He was no longer casting into rise rings (for to do this is to cast into a spot which the fish has left before the fly alights), but midway between the two rings of a cruising fish.

His third cast was answered by the heart-quickening tug which bespeaks a trout grabbing at what he imagines to be a darting nymph. I cannot teach Charles anything about play-ing a fish. My immediate task was done. The hook, I felt, had been well baited, and the victim had risen.

Shortly afterwards, another trout took the nymph and was duly netted. 'Good nymphing, Charles,' I said, noting that there was now a definite gleam in his eye. 'That's two-thirds of your limit, so I expect you want to try a floater for the last one.' The gymnastics were nearly over. The pond had gone comparatively quiet, denoting that the fish were now going to concentrate on flies for the last ten minutes or so.

Charles looked strangely undecided. 'Will they still take a nymph?' he asked. The question was so unexpected that I nearly fell off the catwalk that spans the weir. 'They might, if you play it in the surface film, with just the tiniest twitch now and again.'

He did so, and sure enough the third trout came to his net, giving a total of just over 60oz, which may seem a midget weight by some standards, but a 1¼ lb trout in perfect condition from this pool is very good eating.

Over supper we discussed the technique of casting midway between an observed beat, and I felt I had persuaded him that under pool conditions, where the aim is to induce a rise, this was almost as good as casting to a rising fish.

But I somehow sensed that the chalk stream flowed between us. When next we met it was on his stream. Trout were nymphing with that steady resolve that resists all the blandishments of up-winged copies. The evening was fading. The rise could not last much longer. But Charles was back to his bad old habits. On his cast an Orange Quill moved fitfully in the breeze. Like all his flies, it was beautifully tied, yet as it wavered in that evening-scented air it seemed the embodiment of forlorn hope.

Did I detect upon Charles's calm countenance just the faintest flicker of doubt? If so, it was belied by his voice: 'I am expecting the Blue Winged Olive,' he said.

It was not an explanation; it was an almost Horatian pronouncement. Soon there appeared on the water 'large and violent kidney-shaped whorls'. The Orange Quill became the embodiment of brightest hope. Charles smiled the secret smile of one who knows, and knows that he knows.

CHAPTER 14

A Movable Feast

TIMES CHANGE but seasons merely vacillate. In 1867 Francis Francis wrote; 'In Devon, the trout do not, to my thinking, get into anything like good fettle until they have had a gorge upon that excellent and valuable insect the March Brown. In many rivers they are hardly in fair condition in May, and often not until June, when they have fed upon the Mayfly. After this they are in the primest order, and require all the angler's skill to take them; but they will repay him for his trouble.'

Thirty years later G. A. B. Dewar concluded that 'only in very forward seasons are trout ready for the creel until May is with us'. Both men were writing mainly about wild fish, but a trout is still a trout and, whether native to a water or introduced to it, it probably reacts in much the same way to conditions that encourage or discourage early growth.

I see from my diary that in 1969 the season was delayed. Many brown trout put into ponds at 10in had not reached the acceptable minimum length of 11in by opening date, while rainbows often found it difficult to achieve the 12 in minimum stipulated by some river authorities. Even so, I heard of eager fishermen hooking over ten brace in the first week of April, of which no specimens were takeable. Discretion would have have been the better part of valour in a season preceded by weeks of weather obviously not conducive to good early growth.

Stew-raised trout newly introduced are strong and healthy, and theoretically able to fend for themselves when taken from the stews and put elsewhere, and they soon accept the change from a semi-artificial to a natural environment. But fending for themselves does not always imply bettering themselves. Between the two environments there are certain differences, some of which lead to a temporary cessation of growth.

Water temperature is a basic factor. The temperature of ponds I studied during February and March 1969, after trout had been put in, remained around 40°F almost up to opening day on 1 April. This level is more suitable for spawning than for feeding at a rate that will encourage growth. The fish are taking enough to keep them going but hardly enough to make them grow, and if the result of their feeding is simply to maintain the *status quo*, then one cannot expect sporting-size fish by opening day.

After the spoon-fed security of the stews the need to work hard for their daily bread, chiefly by grubbing about for pond-bed fauna, must take it out of the trout. Anyone sinful enough to catch a trout in winter would find a diet composed of such things as shrimps, snails, water lice and mud-inhabiting larvae like those of caddis flies. All are good food but their finding requires effort and, if this has to be made in a water temperature below that necessary for growth stimulation, then the fish will be doing little more than keeping themselves afloat.

Those I saw hooked at the start of the 1969 season had scarcely got beyond this stage. Relative to their size they were in good fettle, and they put up the resistance of which they were capable. But all their somewhat shamefaced captors had to do was to reel them in, as they might have reeled in driftwood. The fish might as well have been reeled out of the stew pond for all the fishing they offered.

Trout whose feeding in late winter has been sufficient merely to maintain their weight will be hungry by the start of the season. They will take anything the angler chucks at them, from a bunch of wild garlic from the pond-side to something resembling H. T. Sheringham's infamous bottle brush to which, on a day when nothing went right, he resorted in desperation and 'dragged about the river in a half-hearted way'. So fascinated were the trout by this device that sixteen 'of excellent size' fell victims, after which it was consigned to that indecent obscurity which Sheringham considered its due.

Too early catching of trout is a stupid business. No skill is involved; the fish are hooked to no purpose, which must affront them greatly; they can hardly bring satisfaction to the angler; they have to be handled when they should not be; and, as a final insult, they are often flung back as though the flinger were feeding bread to the ducks.

Even where larger trout are put in and the growth factor is less relevant, it is still a poor thing to start too early. Admittedly fish of this size may be takeable but, at the start of a season preceded by cold conditions, they demand little more skill in catching than do the smaller ones. They are more difficult to play, but that is about all.

Fly-fishing clubs are springing up like mushrooms did before the fields were choked with chemicals. One mourns the mushrooms but welcomes the clubs, for the surest safeguard against the itching fingers of those who would scratch away at whatever they imagine to be a 'privileged' sport is for that sport to become popular. But popularity can easily breed poor standards.

When Francis passed his judgement he also said: 'It is the custom in many rivers to commence fly fishing for trout as early as February or March. No doubt the trout being hungry feed better then, but they can hardly be said to be in such condition as the angler loves to see them.'

Condition means not only quality. It includes the ability of the fish to exert such powers of judgement as nature has endowed it with, to lead the angler a dance and, when hooked, to display a determination to give its assailant a full run for his money. It is the stage at which the fish has a fighting chance and the fisherman a chance to prove himself worthy of the fight. The trout that is clobbered almost before it has learnt the difference between pellets and pond olives is less of a poor fish than the man who clobbers it.

Angling clubs can hardly adjust their opening dates at the whims of the weather, but there is nothing to stop anglers from holding back for a time when the fish have clearly had little chance to reach the minimum size. Even this size is rarely indicative of truly sporting fish.

Trout are contrary creatures. Records exist of their feeding and growing in water temperatures below that regarded as optimum for early spring growth. They may have been a special strain, and possibly compensating and energising factors not yet discovered were involved. But the angler's best guide is still a thermometer and, if the water temperature throughout the period of the trouts' introduction has been below 45°F, fish put in at 10in will generally not have reached fighting size.

CHAPTER 15

Teachers and Preachers

A YEAR or two ago there was lively correspondence in the fishing press on the subject of learning to cast a fly. Some correspondents were all for teaching themselves but this, understandably enough, did not receive the unqualified blessing of professional teachers, some of whom advanced cogent arguments in favour of professional tuition.

I turned to G. A. B. Dewar who, in his *Book of the Dry Fly*, caused the placid surface of the pond at Fred Shaw's famous fly-casting school to break out into agitated waves.

'For my part,' wrote Dewar, 'I am inclined to believe that the best way to become an accomplished dry-fly fisherman is to steer clear of teachers and preachers, either in the book, or in the flesh, get down to the water, look out for rising trout, and hammer away until one is at length hooked and landed.'

Sometimes I think Dewar was right, yet when I visit the Game Fair and watch that almost miraculous casting of international or world champions, I think he was wrong. Then I remember Skues who, when tempted to take lessons, always said to himself, 'No, no, my son. Let well alone. You may catch a trout now and then with your amateur, anyhow, hugger-mugger style. If you took lessons and acquired perfection you might catch none'.

Teachers in the book, all worthy men and full of good intentions, can pave the way, if not to hell, then to a fair imitation of purgatory; though if this be the region in which the taught reside, it is usually because they have learnt too grimly, misapplying the teacher's principles. For one such despairing soul, enmeshed in the coils of his casting, salvation lay in a few moments of watching a good caster, without realising that he was being deliberately taught.

This beginner had fallen into an unholy mess, flinging his line back with such gusto that it was impossible to check his rod. The line dropped into the bushes behind him or flopped, exhausted from its punishment, in tangles on the water at his feet.

A nearby angler who could no longer bear the performance or the profanity wandered up and said: 'That's a nice-looking rod. How does it feel?' At which the demented learner, after disentangling himself, reeled in and offered the rod, replying a little sheepishly: 'Not too bad, but a bit stiff for me.'

The angler made three or four beautiful casts, the line rolling out sweetly and straight, the fly kissing the water. The tyro observed secretly but well. This man did not hurl the line behind him with such force that the rod went over with it, but flicked it back with no fuss, barely using his forearm. The rod came alive; the forward cast, made at that exact moment when the line tugged on the rod, was a light, controlled sweep, followed through until the forearm was nearly parallel with the water.

Revelation came in those few moments. The novice learnt, as perhaps he would never have learnt from books, the difference between casting and thrashing. The errors in style, the needless energy, were made plain. Within hours his casting became respectable; within weeks it was good. Two seasons later, it was excellent. And he never realised he had been the subject of a successful confidence trick.

The angler handed back the rod, smiled as sweetly as he had cast, remarked on the rod's virtues and, being a man of tact, made himself scarce. Dewar's advice would have brought this beginner little joy. Perhaps the mistakes would eventually have been overcome, but not without the expense of much time and at the cost of many pounds per square inch of rising blood pressure. Perhaps they would not have been completely overcome, for it is a precept of casting teachers that early mistakes tend to stick.

Skues's 'anyhow, hugger-mugger style' was as near perfect as any self-taught man could hope to achieve. He was a law unto himself, but his remarks on acquiring perfection had a strong general relevance, if by perfection we mean an unfailing ability to lay on the water a dead straight line and cast.

I know a fisherman who is a joy to behold; his actions are so co-ordinated as to seem almost robot-like, and if that suggests something inhuman it is a wrong description, for there is nothing inhuman about him, and everything of graceful movement about his casting. But he is too good; he cannot cast a crooked line. On calm water he is a wizard; where there is drag he remains a novice.

I suspect that Skues had such a peril in mind, though he need not have worried, for he knew every trick. For my part, if I may adapt Dewar, I am inclined to believe that the best way to become an accomplished caster is to steer towards a good teacher. The best one I ever knew was a poacher. He too, taught not by preaching, but by precept.

CHAPTER 16

Fred Shaw:
Fisherman Extraordinary

FRED SHAW'S reaction to the somewhat uncomplimentary opinion of casting teachers implied in Dewar's statement was distinctly snifty. 'Such mentors might just as well advise an absolute novice at cricket to don pads and face the bowling and fielding of an Australian eleven, and slog away until he has made a century.'

One senses a certain hastily applied analogy, some degree of upset to the equilibrium of the normally poised Shaw. After all, Dewar's novice flycaster *will* eventually land a fish. If Shaw's novice batsman will eventually make a century, will that not be an unexampled achievement? Imagine the coverage today; the Hampdenshire Wonder come alive, with bat instead of ball, a certainty for the Honours List, a cricket column guaranteed for life, an autobiography with advance excerpts in the *Sunday Times*. And last, but certainly not least, the commentator swallowing his microphone.

Fred G. Shaw, FGS, was a man of many accomplishments; angler, angling writer, inventor and designer of fisherman's needs, amateur casting champion and a pioneer of the modern fly-fishing schools. He had globe-trotted nearly everywhere and had fished many of the world's fresh waters.

One of my most cherished boyhood gifts, long since gone into limbo, had been handed down, via my father, from the designer himself. It was a Fisherman's Knife and though it had been used regularly by my father for perhaps ten years or more, it was still in first-class condition. It was ¼in thick, 4in long, weighed 2oz, and contained 'the eight necessary tools of the fly fisherman': disgorger, lancet, scissors, file, nippers, screwdriver, stiletto and blade. Along its handle was engraved a measure with hook sizes.

The stiletto was needle sharp, excellent for poking wax out of hook eyes or, in the wrong hands, for poking into other small boys. The file was four-sided, and ended in the disgorger. The scissors were spring-loaded, surgical in quality. Every item was magnetic and so would immediately extract the desired fly from the box.

The steel was best Sheffield. In those days there was no nonsense about Continental steel; nothing could beat Sheffield. At 10s 6d (it had gone up 3s in eight years) there was probably no neater, or finer combination of such tools in pocket-knife form to be had anywhere. My model was nickel-handled; for 15s the knife handle was in ivory, or for £1 1s in silver.

Apart from *The Science of Dry Fly Fishing*, 1906, and *The Complete Science of Fly Fishing and Spinning*, 1914, Shaw wrote such improbable works as *Comets and Their Tails*, *The Gegenschein Light*, *Fiscal Facts and Fictions*. Presumably somebody read these, though perhaps remaining as baffled as some of his reviewers appeared to be. Of the first named, *Nature*, evidently shy of getting embroiled, said: 'The work as a whole is brief; its tone is very modest', which must have shown in a nicely retiring light the man who had earlier advanced an 'ingenious solution of the great geological puzzle of the Witwatersrand Conglomerates'.

To us there is something almost bizarre about a school for salmon and trout fly casting, complete with casting lawn and pool, 'about ten minutes by taxi' from Piccadilly Circus. Nevertheless, there it was, at 5 Marlborough Road, St John's Wood, an 'extensive and exclusively private coaching ground,' set off by handsome trees and containing an equally handsome residence. It began in 1906 and within eight years Mr Shaw had 'perfected the fly casting of over 2,000 clients, including a great number of Ladies, Officers in His Majesty's Naval and Military Forces, School Boys and well-known public men'. Priorities were more defined in 1914; public men, bless them, had not yet rated capitals.

From his pupils an imposing stream of congratulations issued forth, to be duly recorded in his brochures by the delighted proprietor. On 1 August 1907, from The Most Hon The Marquis of ——: 'I cannot thank you too much for all the trouble you took with me; you have certainly increased my pleasure tenfold.' From the Hon George P—— on 22 June 1908: 'Allow me to express my sense of your admirable capacities as a teacher, and of the remarkable speed with which you can instil the principles of the art of which you are a master.'

There was 'A Member Of The Diplomatic Service', and 'A Well Known Traveller' who wrote from the Wyndham Club. The former seems to have been not only diplomatic but also a visionary, for after his lessons he assured his teacher that 'the result has made fishing a lifelong pleasure for me'. From 'A Well-Known Singer' (Plunket Greene?) on 14 March 1912, recording a fishing trip: 'I never had a blank day the whole time I was there—my average was eight fish a day averaging between ¾lb to 1½lb. I must say that I chiefly owed my success to your excellent tuition.'

Fred Shaw was cast in the heroic mould. For him it was all or nothing. *The Fishing Gazette*, the *Country Gentleman*, the *Morning Post*, *Daily Express*, *Angler* and *Scottish Field* were invited to attend the piscatorial jollifications ten minutes from Piccadilly Circus, and to commit their amazement irrevocably to print.

Having for years used a piece of apple rootstock with its graft union shaped into a knob for administering the last rites, I feel it would be nice to have Shaw's 'Ephemeridae'

Fly Catching Net and Priest, notwithstanding the dubious connection between priest and *ephemeridae*. This was a combination of priest and net handle (most ingenious, said the *Fishing Gazette* of 20 May 1906). It was telescopic, measuring 42in when extended, 12in when closed. In the latter position it would take the net for short-arm work, being then 18in overall. It weighed 7oz and cost 21s with spare net. Also costing 21s was the inexhaustible Mr Shaw's Fishing Creel, of best English cane and with best quality straps and nickel fittings. This was no ordinary creel. It combined a luncheon basket and a separate compartment for the fish. These were slid through an aperture to lie flat on a false bottom beneath the sandwiches. A lid opened from the fish compartment for extraction of its contents. The fish thus went in at the top and came out at the bottom. The creel was lockable.

Complete with neck lanyard, price 7s 6d, postage 3d, was the Fisherman's Lamp, 'portable, steady and self-contained. No liquid to spill, and perfectly safe with petrol'. The illustration shows a night angler knotting on a fly in the powerful beam of the lamp. Here, Shaw's sense of the dramatic was a little overdone; the angler comes out as a shifty-looking cove, who might be a burglar examining a stolen brooch.

There was the Oil Box for oiling flies, with lid showing the great man in action, and there were the 'Inimitable' Fishing Spectacles, hinged affairs that worked from side-buttons on the cap, 'always safe, always ready, always convenient'. When not in use they were kept on 'the peak of the fishing cap, the fez, smoking cap etc'.

Shaw's masterpiece was his Dry Fly Rod, 9ft 6in, with butt spear, spare top and leather-capped bamboo case, at four-and-a-half guineas. 'Most perfectly finished', said Lord Hotham, or 'a little beauty', as Mrs N. Leslie wrote, enclosing her cheque. Some people, including Shaw, said that it rivalled the famous Leonard.

One look at that impressive portrait, and we see a man disdainful of the shoddy. Nothing that Shaw made fell to bits. He fashioned well; he made things to last. We could do with him today.

CHAPTER 17

Greenheart and Cane

I NEVER had the luck to own a Shaw fly rod. My first weapon
was a greenheart. For sheer beauty in a fishing rod it would
be hard to beat greenheart, and the man who regards the
term 'inanimate' as a libel on anything fashioned from wood,
must see greenheart as an example of life adorned with
excellence. Perhaps it was this sense of fitness that moved a
stable boy employed by my grandfather to wave the latter's
new rod in the air and to announce, 'I wisht I could try this
rod'. At which its owner implied that it was indeed likely to
be tried, but not in a manner usually associated with fishing.
Judging by the great brass-mounted contemporary that came
down to me, the new weapon would have been ideal for such
a dual purpose. As an admirer of the Canon of Westminster,
my grandfather was doubtless following that good man's
advice to the angler 'to get himself a stiff and powerful rod,

whereby he will obtain after some weeks of aching muscles a fore-arm fit for a sculptor's model, and trout hooked and killed, instead of pricked and lost'.

By 1926 greenheart was as wandlike as it is today. From the Junior Army & Navy Stores you could get a 9ft, 3-joint model of 8oz, which was only an ounce heavier than my modern two-piece, while similar versions were sold by Harrods and Gamages.

A correspondent recalled recently how, as a rod-maker's apprentice in 1903, it was his job to visit the local horse and carriage works to procure old hansom cab greenheart shafts from which the lads had to cut by hand lengths of 1in, ½in, and ¼in square for rod making. With over sixty years of craftsmanship behind him, my correspondent believes that not even split cane can approach 'the wonderful feel of uninterrupted flow from arm through wrist and rod butt to rod tip and line of those old rods'.

And what other wood, save perhaps lance wood and hickory, could serve the lifetime of a hansom cab and then be made into a fishing rod? Yet in spite of its toughness, greenheart may split along the grain of the top portion, where the action is broken, however slightly, by the ferrule. But I suspect that much of the breaking and laziness to which greenheart is allegedly prone was due to heavy handling and the hauling out of sunken lines.

I never fish a sunk line with greenheart; fishing a sunken line means that you must either pull line out of the water to re-cast or else retrieve all but the cast. The first is too much of a strain, the second means false casting, which if done continually is asking too much of this wood. My own rod is reserved specifically for a sunk cast on a floating line, and used thus it is first rate for wet-fly work.

I do not like it for dry-fly fishing, or perhaps it is the rod that does not like me. My own preference for the dry fly is always a fairly stiff cane. Reel and line weight are possibly even more important for greenheart than for cane. The relatively heavy greenheart needs some degree of counter-balancing by a reel somewhat heavier than one would use for split cane. My latest 9ft greenheart—which is half an ounce lighter than the same length of cane in three pieces—takes a 3¼in reel and a floating line of AFTM 6. It would take five and still send it out, but seven is just that shade too heavy.

The makers of my spliced-cane rod evidently do not believe in hiding their talents, for they assure me that theirs are without doubt the best rods it is possible to purchase. Since my mania for rod buying has not yet embraced every specimen in existence I cannot argue the point, but as far as my experience goes, there is nothing to touch this magnificent tool for dry-fly work. A lifetime of carefree fishing is promised me by the enthusiastic manufacturers, which would have been wonderful had it come forty years ago. All I pray is that when the rod is finally handed down it will not end up as my grandfather's did, which was to be given to the local sweep as handles for his chimney brushes.

In its ability to provide unbroken movement the spliced rod has always been superior to the ferruled, and its re-introduction in these days of improved binding materials is a welcome recognition of the fact. When the tape is removed, it is sometimes found that tiny shreds of fibre stick to the material, but I am reliably informed that these are not 'root fibres' but merely minute deposits left after the smoothing process. Nevertheless, care is always needed when untaping. Some people prefer to leave the rod made up for the season, but this frequently necessitates rod clips on one's car, and of all the misguided aids to fishing yet devised out of the goodness of somebody's heart, car rod-clips are high on the list. If the rod is laid along the roof it will sooner or later get smashed into a wall, or its tip or butt will disappear into the maw of some monstrous lorry snorting six inches behind.

If it is fixed either vertically or obliquely to clips on the side of the car it will get whipped about in the windstream. Some people treat a rod almost like a walking-stick and get away with it, but I am one of those unfortunate males who carry a fishing rod as expertly as they carry a baby; in both cases disaster is never far away, so where rods are concerned I like to give the demons of disaster the least possible opportunity.

It is often claimed that two-piece rods have a less interrupted action than three-piece. I think this is true of the spliced rod when measured against the three-piece ferruled. In my view the former is the nearest to the complete flow that one might expect, in theory, from a single tapered length of 9ft, if such a thing existed, but to me there is usually a joint disturbance in the ferruled rod, whether cane or greenheart. As Skues put it, 'They always seem to have a bone in the middle'. This is possibly less evident with the stiffest type of cane, but beyond a certain limit stiffness becomes wearying.

The brook rod, symbol of freedom among mountain streams and unrenowned brooks far from the world's hideous clatter, is the sweetest of them all. Though a mere toy to the loch and reservoir angler, it is, in fact, in the right hands, capable of dealing with fish much larger than the average brook specimen, and will bring to the net with complete equanimity, trout of 2lb and more. There are stories of salmon being handled on a brook rod; such handling I have not seen, but I have known a 3¼lb trout brought in on one.

A brook rod of top grade cane is an example of 'power-weight ratio' at its most perfect, the maximum possible length, making for feather-light casting and feather-light but firm striking. Experts, of whom I am not one, can cast practically the same amount of line as the average performer can cast with a nine-footer. If I were strong-willed enough to limit myself to one rod for all floating line work on brook, river and pool, my choice would be the brook rod, complete mastery of which in all conditions would be a signal achievement.

It is not my presumption, nor within my capacity, to set up as an adviser on rods. I merely draw on my experience, which may be quite different from that of others. The rod of one of the most accomplished casters I know feels to me like a shepherd's crook.

I admire the faith of those fishing writers who advise testing rod and line before buying, rather than merely waggling the rod about in the shop. It is admirable in theory, but many tackle shops are a long way from testing grounds and I cannot see dealers in these sorrowful times letting a chance customer loose with £20 or £30's worth of temptation in his hands. Perhaps the best plan would be to invite the dealer and his rods to lunch.

CHAPTER 18

Days of Perch and Dace

EDMUND BLUNDEN, who was a fisherman as well as a poet, wrote of 'the ogling hunch-back perch with needled fin', a neat description that implies the dandy, which this fish of gorgeous raiment certainly is. I think, however, that he pursues with gastronomic rather than amorous intent; his affections lie not for the fair sex, but for his own stomach. Like most dandies, he is very sure of himself. Not for him the sombre mantle and lurking stealth of the pike; he runs riot, with colours flying.

He is a fish that has fed at least one king and his queen, for at Winchester in 1403 Henry IV and Joan of Navarre partook of 'Tench embrace, Troutez and Perchys', thereby showing themselves to be epicures in the grand manner. Both the perch, and the often maligned tench, are fish of flavour, if they are not ruined by those mysterious coagulants known as 'garnishings'.

Perch are healing, purifying fish, said the writers of old. Two little bones in the head were a remedy for the 'stone', or as Izaak Walton has it, 'very medicinable against the stone in the reins'. Their flesh was good for wounded soldiers and women in child-bed, and long before chemicals were poured into the Rhine, the perch of that river were the yardstick of wholesome food.

Into the marital affairs of perch no family planners have poked their inquisitorial noses, or, if they have, those unpleasant appendages have been well and truly bitten off. The fecundity of the female must be accounted one of nature's irresistible forces. Picot, the Swiss biologist, claimed that a quarter of the weight of a pound perch he opened was composed of the ovary with its 992,000 eggs. Later estimates have been more modest: 127,240 eggs in a 2lb 11oz fish, 155,620 in one of 3lb, 280,000 in another of 1½lb. Safety in numbers, and even in spite of often enormous mortality, enough eggs hatch to enable perch to maintain their admirable traditions of community life, which frequently involve eating each other, a much more dignified way of beating the population explosion than submitting to family planners.

When I recall the exploits of my fishing companion of childhood I sometimes wonder at all the injunctions to the perch fisher. Unlike Sir William Davenant's angler, he took for angling-rod not a sturdy oak, but a sturdy ash; some thin water cord, a few feet of gut and a bottle-cork float. With this lavish gear and a tin of worms he landed perch after perch. But how art was concealed, and what a nose that boy had! He seldom picked dead water or a shoal of small fish. Appropriately, he was known as Perce.

Perce knew next to nothing, and probably cared less, about the artistry of casting. Name dropping was lost on him. Mention that your dad knew Hutton, and Perce merely murmured absently: 'Oo's 'e, mate?' Fishing was not a game, but a serious business; times were hard, Perce was one of six and they were a hungry lot. In retrospect I have to admit that young Perce's playing of his fish showed little delicacy. He simply lifted up his ash pole and swung the victim on to the bank, but even that ignominious procedure must have had no small measure of skill, for he hardly ever dropped his catch. And if Perce did have a twinge of conscience, it was stilled by the thought of those rumbling stomachs at home.

For me it has always been the fly, if you can call an Alexandra a fly, as a chalk-stream friend mumbled one day when I took him to my perch pond. But fly or lure, what could be prouder than a touch of peacock feather? And there is a nice poetic justice in setting a dandy to catch a dandy, as I am sure Edmund Blunden would have agreed.

Perch are no easy game. They are fish of brains as well as beauty. If the fly is wrongly worked, a man may fiddle for hours and not get a single take. The youngsters are rash with the splendid rashness of innocence, coming time and again at a nymph in a trout pool where they have no business to be, but with age comes wisdom and wariness, together with a disdain of trifles. The big fish are out for the fry and the minnows, darting objects that cannot be simulated by the steady monotonous retrieve. It is the light twitch that does the trick, with a big fly cast into the ripples round a reed bed, and fairly well sunk, since perch never come to the surface. There is only one effective variation I know of, which is the really fast retrieve.

Perch take the fly with a bang. There is none of that nosing around a worm which caused Izaak Walton to give 'but this advice, that you give the Perch time enough when he bites; for there was scarce ever any angler that has given him too much'. But the hold is usually light, and rough handling will lose the fish. They are lusty quarry, game to the last, when they fix you with an eye no longer ogling, but glittering with fury, as they raise that needled fin.

Perce never fumbled those blood-letting spines. A quick

grab with the left-hand finger and thumb, and the fin was helpless. Then a smart clout, and one more fish was ready for Mum's scaling knife.

Then there were dace, in the dog days of July and August, when trout had gone comatose, and when my companion and mentor was my old parson friend.

'Keep it short, m'boy,' he said, sound advice at any time, which he followed to the letter. He called it the rule of ten: a ten-minute sermon, a ten-foot line, a ten-inch trout. And he called dace the poor man's trout. 'Very appropriate,' he sighed, and he sighed more truly than I, rich with the plunder of boyhood, could hope to understand.

Eventually, I caught some dace. The parson patted me on the head. 'Get your mother to broil 'em dry, with a pat of butter. Francis Francis, y'know,' he mused; then musing still further, 'can't think why the feller said "don't forget the bacon rind".' He met my wondering gaze a little sorrowfully: 'to bait the fly with.'

Years later I came across another old gentleman in Normandy. He had a whitewashed farmhouse, a few apple trees and a silvery stream. In that stream were trout and dace. In August he would dig up caddis larvae from the stream bed, complete with their covering of debris. These floated on the end of the line and were readily taken by dace. He called them *porte-bois*, and said his grandfather taught him the trick.

All my life I have loved the happy little quicksilver dace, the shapeliest fish I know. He is never sulky, but always ready to have a go, whether at a nymph, Pheasant Tail, Blue Upright or Black Gnat. His taste is catholic, but not indiscriminate. He is no gourmet, yet neither is he a glutton. An easygoing chap but not one to be bamboozled by a pretentious menu.

For toning up the reflexes there is no fish like him in British waters, for he will take and eject quicker than a blink of the angler's eyelids, hence the recommendation for bacon rind and various other baits, a form of angling which leaves me appalled at the lengths to which even great men like Francis would go.

Dace live in shoals, and the job is to take them swiftly and quietly from the tail end with a very short line. Given too much rope, they will not hang themselves; they will leave the angler not only fishless, for the fish will nearly always slip off, but also with empty water, because the commotion will send the shoals 20 or 30 yards upstream. It will then be necessary to wait a good ten minutes to let them settle.

The trouble with these delightful fish is that they just will not know their place. No forelock pulling for them, no humble self-effacement, not even a tentative withdrawing from the presence of gentry. They are not content with the rich man's crumbs, but will pinch the dinner from his plate, and the plate as well if he doesn't look out. Their manners really are deplorable. Evidently no dace ever went to Winchester.

CHAPTER 19

Game or Gamin?

ON A bright winter's day when the air is like chilled cider—
and I mean real cider, not the apology of the London pubs—
and the sun melts the frost upon the grass and glints upon the
steely riffles of the Lugg, I will not hear a word against the
grayling. A coarse fish, indeed! does he not belong to the
noble family of salmon and trout? *Thymallus thymallus*; the
very name is a poem, a cadence, the most perfect two-word
rhyme ever written. Speak it softly; see how sweetly it slips
from the tongue. Yet could it rise to heights of affirmation,
enshrined in some glorious credo. And sweet is the flesh of
this most subtly coloured fish.

'Nor (newly taken) more the curious taste doth please,'
wrote Michael Drayton, completing the couplet somewhat
ungallantly:

'The grayling, whose great spawn is big as any pease.'

My companion on the Itchen was less enthusiastic as we
peered one day into its crystal depths. 'Grayling,' he snorted,

'the devil take them.' But the devil was fishing in more profitable waters and heeded us not.

On that particular occasion I, too, consigned the grayling to perdition, thereby exhibiting a woeful inconsistency. That is the trouble with those of us who are both trout and grayling fishers. In his rightful place we revere him as a worthy quarry, as game in both senses as trout, or nearly so. In his wrongful place we revile him as a gamin, a river urchin, a greedy pestilential, interfering busybody, and a bully to boot. In spite of which, I heard recently of someone who had actually introduced grayling into a trout stream. What execration would descend upon those go-getting imperialists, those ruthless colonisers of other peoples' territory, those usurpers of thrones and dynasties! Cats would more readily lie down with pigeons than grayling with trout.

Who but an incorrigible romantic could have named this thrusting fish The Lady of the Stream? A brawny wench, I'm thinking, a very Amazon. I have not yet detected any lady-like reticence or dainty table manners among hen grayling, and whatever the cock may be, he is certainly not effeminate. A curious misnomer, is it not, and one that places a pretty fancy before elementary biology. But that, alas, is the way with romantics. Ausonious, the Roman poet, was more credible with his 'bright scaled umber'. There we note the professional touch.

It is odd that the grayling's lightning strike up from the deeps has been emphasised in fishing literature almost to the exclusion of the deadly forward move to intercept an on-coming fly. This movement I take to be a compensating factor to make up for the frequent mistiming of the upward lunge. Every grayling fisher knows how the fish will come belting up to the Red Tag, which its ultra-keen eye can hardly fail to see, only to miss it perhaps three times out of four. But the forward glide, and it is seldom more than a glide, and hardly ever a lunge, pinpoints the fly nearly every time, and takes by surprise the angler who is expecting only the upward charge.

It is almost as though nature, having endowed the fish with a most penetrating eye, a wide field of vision, and a large and powerful dorsal fin to provide speed, realised that she had somehow failed to relate vision and speed to judgement, and so made amends before it was too late. I have watched grayling for hours on end feeding in chalk streams, where their every motion was clearly visible, and have noticed that in the summer far more surface food was taken from only just below than from deep down. In summer and autumn they lie in shallower water anyway. The actual take is certainly a snap, and can easily give the impression of a short charge and snap combined, whereas it is more likely to be either a short glide ending in a snap, or a short, sharp upward turn.

In winter the lunge from the bottom is more evident; the fish go to deeper water and lie low, but there are several weeks of grayling fishing when the fish are still in comparatively shallow water. During this period I try to put out of my mind the much publicised upward charge, and to anticipate the other kind of take.

The strange thing about the grayling is that such a refined creature has such catholic tastes. The trout is an epicure, sometimes to the point of disdain (*pace* the DSIR which in 1935 stated, 'brown trout feed indiscriminately on any convenient animal organism'). Not so the grayling, who will often take almost any insect that comes its way, though it does not often stoop to eating other fish. This omnivorous habit is a boon to anglers, for there are numerous imitations that will succeed.

The primary factor as regards tackle is, I think, a fine cast, made necessary by the grayling's very keen eyesight. There is a 4¾lb breaking-strain cast of 0·008in on the market which I like, but people more skilled would prefer 3½lb or even 3lb breaking strain. A biggish grayling returning to the deeps can snap light tackle on the first dive. Furthermore, since a No 2 hook is the very largest—often size o is the ideal—and as lip-hooked grayling are easily lost, any jerk on the downward plunge can be fatal. I do not like a slack cast on the water, unless drag has to be overcome, but I do like slack line in the left hand to take up the initial shock.

To my mind the playing of the fish is a compromise between giving it just enough rope and giving it too much. When it has dived, which occurs in less time than it takes the angler to think about it, the game must stop, and the fish must be hustled. Give a grayling a chance and it will roll, plunge and cavort like a boisterous puppy. It may not fight as long as a trout will, but it has more tricks, and if it goes to weed, it will fray the fine cast to shreds. Dexterity in handling grayling lies not so much in playing the fish, but in landing it before it has had a chance to play the angler. This may seem unsporting, but there are many, many slips between the net and the grayling's lip. The net is often the final one. The sight of a landing-net sends a grayling berserk. Just when you think all is over it will go like a torpedo, and then there really will be fun and games, for after the first round the fish will prove its pugnacity in furious style.

The cunning take from the near-surface glide demands a strike of the utmost accuracy, for which a tight line is vital, but again with slack ready to hand. There is a fraction of time between the entry of the fly and its ejection. If it goes just far enough for the hook to reach the jaw, and if the strike is made then, the fish will at least be tethered. But more often than not, owing probably to the small mouth, which must be sensitive to the artificial, the fly is either rejected or else the hook goes into the lip. If several takes like this occur and the fish are lost the best plan is to use a slightly larger hook. Casting downstream is sometimes more successful, as regards the actual take, than casting up. Upstream casting can line the fish, particularly as grayling occur in shoals, which makes it difficult to cast upstream without covering at least some fish with the cast, if not with line. With the downstream cast slack line is also needed, as the ideal is to cast a few feet upstream of the shoal and to let the fly drift down. Downstream work does of course make hooking more difficult, since the strike pulls the fly away from the fish.

One must more or less forget trout tactics when fishing for grayling, except for basic considerations of concealment and delicacy of presentation. For one thing, when a trout misses a fly, at least on placid water, it is usually deliberate, either through epicurean disdain or an instinctive awareness of danger. But when the lunging grayling misses through an error of judgement, he may come again and yet again at the same fly, so it is bad policy to remove the fly and recast immediately after the first miss. Leave it to float, and it may well be taken seconds afterwards.

In the matter of fly life I prefer to be as pernickety as possible because I think it greatly adds interest; but this does not always work, and there are times when a Red Tag, Red Ant, Tup's or Greenwell's will do far more good than a natural imitation. As my housemaster said to me on the occasion of my coming top of the form—a freak event never to be repeated—what man has done, man can do, and if I catch one grayling on a Red Tag I usually manage to catch another on the same fly. Wet-fly work for grayling is quite different from downstream and across angling with flashers for trout. Flashers are not much good, since grayling rarely take fry, so we are confined to nymphs and the like. Casting downstream and across with a long cast greased to within 3 or 4in allows the nymph to be carried about in swirls and eddies in a reasonably lifelike manner, and so long as it is merely twitched when it reaches the end of the cast, and is not forcibly pulled upstream, it will give a fair simulation of the natural.

Nymphing can be very successful in autumn when the fish

are in shallower, swifter water. In winter, when they are in deep, still pools, the floater comes into its own, but if it does not tempt, nymphs should be tried. A floating line is essential; sunk lines simply take the fly below the fishes' feeding zone.

I sometimes think the Itchen grayling must be a breed apart, when compared with those of the Lugg. The fingerlings in the Itchen, at least where I fish, will rise to a dry fly whenever they are feeding, which is very obliging of them, and as they frequently feed at times when trout are simply basking, I spend an hour or two whipping them out, thus helping in some measure to keep the stock down. The middle-size, edible specimens do not come well and truly to the fly until early autumn, while the big brutes that have long outlived edibility won't come to it at all, or to a nymph. To them, nothing but worms or maggots are of any interest.

On the Lugg, all sizes will take dry flies and nymphs, at all events from autumn onwards. Perhaps it is not so much the breed as the water. The rich bottom larder of the Itchen offers food in plenty, and in secure surroundings. The Lugg, being a spate stream, is a barer cupoard. There the fish must have one eye on the deeps and another on the surface.

Which suits me very well. *Thymallus* of the Lugg, I salute you. Long may you flourish.

CHAPTER 20

Izaak Walton Re-Visited

SOME YEARS ago when fishing in Wales, I met an angler whose almost sole concession to modernity was that excellent book, *The Angler's Vade Mecum*, which he had just presented to his wife. After years of the grass-widowhood so unflinchingly endured by non-fishing wives, she had finally taken to the rod, which as she said briskly and in very truth, was better than taking to the bottle, and it looked as though it would have to be one or the other.

My new acquaintance was a man to be respected, committing to perdition fibreglass rods and all such trash, mourning the demise of gut casts, but allowing that nylon lines are the greatest gift in angling history to lazy fishermen.

He had those bright blue eyes behind which lies the faith that is more than Norman blood, proof against the philosophy of fools and the promises of politicians. His lodestar was Izaak Walton. *The Compleat Angler* said all that needed saying; it was the only strictly necessary book in the whole literature of the gentle art. All fishing books were delightful, but they were all cribs from Izaak, including the *Vade Mecum*.

Such devotion would remain steadfast unto death, and doubtless beyond, and if it suggests a blind spot in those bright blue eyes, we all have one somewhere.

For years I have been niggled by a judgement on Walton attributed to a certain Captain Rowland, a bachelor who was 'a worshipful old man, sharp tempered, indolent, yet always occupied, with rosy carbuncled face, who swore freely,' and who lived long years ago in a great old house among the Carmarthenshire hills, 'where he cheated *ennui* with some choice books and a cabinet of teacups'.

Captain Rowland, whose travels were over, now followed the precept that wise men bide at home, and 'was seldom abroad, save to fish, and out of doors he was metamorphosed. He then invariably wore black clothes, a tall silk hat, and a white cravat. He would sit, amid the Hosannahs of Jubilant Nature, as summer passed into the land, like an old tree beside the stream, like a figure in a frieze'.

While he fished, the Captain never spoke a word. 'Fishing is fishing'; there was a time to talk and a time to fish.

Now when such a man does speak, his remarks mean something, and Captain Rowland, though he loved *The Compleat Angler*, would not countenance its author, 'who was first a lover of the picturesque, and merely, in the second place, an angler'.

Those whom the inquities of live-baiting leave aghast at man's inhumanity to minnows, or who shudder at the very thought of maggots, may find Walton's appeal limited mainly to the 'picturesque', but it is one that must surely remain undimmed. From the moment he stretched his legs up Tottenham Hill to his final injunction from Thessalonians, 'Study to be quiet', he spent five days that, in their way, shook the world.

When I consider the heterogeneous communities that inhabit my fly boxes, I think of Walton's advice that, although it may be necessary to 'counterfeit' a particular fly on a particular river, in general, three or four flies 'neat and rightly made and not too big' will serve for trout in most rivers all the summer.

Perhaps they will. My blue-eyed companion of the Elysian week among the tumbling streams of Wales remained faithful to the Waltonian doctrine. The Coachman, Grey Duster, Coch-y-bondhu and Herefordshire Alder were all he asked of life, and a week was enough to show that he knew how to catch trout.

But would Walton have been content with such a meagre

collection if he had known as much about flies as we know today? I rather think he would have delighted in trying to unravel the entomological mysteries of the trout stream, and he did, after all, name twelve flies. Some there are who never venture outside their three or four patterns, or even less. Such singleness of purpose is heroic, but what is missed in the pretty game of fly spotting and in the arts of 'counterfeiting'.

Some of Walton's 'jury of flies likely to betray and condemn all the Trouts in the river' we can still recognise. The first was the dun-fly in March, which suggests the March Brown. His stone-fly for April, had body of black wool, yellow underwings and tail, and wings of drake feathers, though in fact it was not his, but a dressing given by that elusive and perhaps mythological lady, Dame Juliana Berners, in 1496. Early May saw the ruddy-fly, copied with body of red wool wrapped with black silk. This was probably the female spinner of the Iron Blue Dun. The yellow or greenish fly in May sounds like the Olive Dun. The sad yellow-fly of June rather puzzles me; perhaps the Medium Olive, better described, I think, as sad-yellow fly.

Vague he may seem to those reared in the school of exactitude, but he was as meticulous as anyone of his time could be. His Mayflies were 'ribbed with black hair; or some of them ribbed with silver thread', which suggests that he recognised the difference in abdominal markings between dun and spinner, at least of *Ephemera danica*. He remarks on the value of noting what specimens fall on the water, of catching them and tying a copy by the waterside.

'Now you must be sure not to cumber yourself with too long a line, as most do, and have the sun before you; and carry the point of your rod downward, by which means the shadow of yourself, and rod too, will be least offensive to the fish; for the sight of any shade amazes the fish, and spoils your sport.'

Hundreds of angling writers have echoed it, hundreds will echo it yet. But not all anglers abide by it. Some measure distance according to shadow, use a bush for shelter, make obeisance on bended knee. They catch fish. Others stand sun-struck at the river's edge. Coming events cast their shadows before, and fish do not wait upon the coming.

But what is too long for a line? For nymphing in streams, 12 inches beyond the necessary can be too long, and 24 inches of over-length can lose fish after fish, yet 20 or 30 yards may be needed to reach an opposite bank with a dry fly. Charles Cotton, doomed for all eternity to fish just below Walton, was all for 'fine and far-off', which was splendid advice to the downstream man. Did he dream that he had coined a phrase that would tickle the ears of anglers three centuries later?

I cannot quite share the ardour of my blue-eyed companion, who would not remove a single wisp of duskish wool from Izaak's moorish-fly, but I know my desert island will be incomplete without *The Compleat Angler*.

CHAPTER 21

Bank Clearing by Numbers

HAD THERE been a devotee of nature wandering the banks of our trout pool on that sharp winter's morning when a small band bedizened with bill-hooks, slashers, axes and a chain-saw arrived on the scene, he might have been forgiven for imagining that a collection of vandals had erupted bent on reducing sylvania to a state of devastation. Such immediate fears would have been excusable, for the sight of men armed with tools of destruction must cause the heart of many a country dweller to descend into his stomach with a sickening thud.

However, our hypothetical observer need not have worried. We were out not to destroy, but to improve. Ours was to be no haphazard, press-on-regardless operation, but a planned programme of bank clearance based firmly on the fly-casting experience of several seasons. We had clear and definite ends in view; to facilitate casting, to open up thickly shaded areas of water to more sunlight, and to prevent excessive leaf fall with its subsequent fouling of the pond margins.

I had in mind at least one example of the inhibiting effects of dense shade on trout water, where a stream flows for quite long stretches beneath a heavy canopy of alders. Along these stretches there is a marked absence of crowfoot, a most valuable weed for trout, since it harbours several species of *ephemeroptera* nymphs. Stones on the stream bed are virtually bare of the algae also normally colonised by these nymphs, so that as a larder of the type to encourage rising trout, the water is poor, and the fly fisher, whether nymphing or using dry flies, has a thin time. Such trout as do occur are bottom feeders, and there are not many anyway. The amount of summer sunlight reaching the water is probably only some 10–15 per cent of that reaching the more open lengths, where crowfoot and other good weeds grow well, and where the trout are excellent.

I remembered, too, the corpse of a squirrel I once found enmeshed in nylon and hanging from a tree. That unlucky animal must have suffered grievously. Wherever nylon is seen dangling, the twig bespeaks a fly trap and a possible gibbet for squirrels and birds, and I make a point of cutting out with the long-arm pruner all such hazards.

Nothing should so mortify a man engaged on bank clearance as the spectacle of a tree needlessly felled, and to make certain that none of us should have his conscience stricken, we had carefully plotted the area, indicating all trees which were to be left. Just as there are more ways than one of thinning, so there are of casting a fly, and we were no subscribers to the notion that vegetation should always be sacrificed to the convenience of the standard back cast. We did not want to make things too simple, for some people like to sort out the fish that demands the deft flip into the embowered sanctuary, or the unconventional but stylistic switch invented in a moment of inspiration.

Experience of where, and in what circumstances, a fly gets snagged up is the whole basis of efficient thinning. One needs to know which trees, or parts of trees, collect one's flies, which is quite different from merely guessing. Casting knowledge in relation to prevailing winds is of the utmost value, for if one can judge within a foot or two how far the fly is blown off course at a particular point on the bank, or when making a particular type of cast, then one is far better able to decide on the removal or retention of certain branches, or even thin shoots.

Branch or tree removal purely in relation to casting convenience does not necessarily provide for adequate sunlight penetration, but in general it is remarkable how the two go together. I do not say that each is bound to complement the other, but as a rule it does, and it is usually found that if timber removal is related to reasonable casting needs, the question of light on the water will also be answered.

Working on the numbers principle, we cleared out first all the scrub and bramble, burning as we went. This left the place much clearer for the swinging of axes, and possibly saved a severed leg or two, for our task force included clerks and clerics, whose daily tools do not normally comprise such weapons. I recalled the gory tales about forestry novitiates told me years ago by a Sussex woodcutter, and we plumped for safety before valour.

Next came the saplings and dead trees, and finally the very few living trees, mainly alders. Stems of usable size were laid aside, since they always come in useful for bank strengthening or making casting rafts. It has to be accepted that standards of cutting will vary, because axemanship and the skilled use of a bill-hook are not part of everyone's life. When it was all over a friend and I returned to cut off at ground level all those stumps that looked as though they had been chewed off.

Two things stood out when the job was finally accomplished. One was that in spite of seemingly mountainous amounts of cut material we had removed practically nothing of value to the waterside landscape. The other was that we had actually improved the scene to a marked extent. To such an extent that when I arrived for my first evening rise of the season I found two boys all set up with sandwiches and spinning gear. By what mysterious grapevine the news had reached those youngsters in their home town nearly twenty miles away I did not discover. They had come by bus to the nearest village and had walked the two miles to the pool. Both assured me that we had made a jolly good job of the clearing, and one offered me ginger beer.

Bank clearance is all too often regarded as just a job for the lads to let off steam. As a steam-letting exercise it is certainly first rate, and as a steaming-up one, hard to beat. But it also demands considerable planning and real care in execution. Indeed, it is almost a rural craft, no less so than controlled scrub clearance or woodland felling.

It is essentially a compromise between the anglers' needs and the bankside environment, a matter of striking a balance that satisfies the former without violating the latter. Unhappily, examples exist where no thought has been given to such a policy, but where everything along the water's edge has been mercilessly hacked out, greatly to the detriment not only of the landscape, but also to the wild life it once sustained, much of which, ironically enough, comprised creatures like sedges and alder flies, which are indispensable to the fly-fishing scene.

A trout pool is not a reservoir but a comparatively small area of water having an essentially secluded and intimate atmosphere. It is not a place for the long-haulers shooting out forty yards of line, but one offering a variety of techniques to catch fish that may be choosing from a much wider food range than is often thought. Pond olive nymphs, chironomid pupae, sedges, black gnats, water boatmen and certain duns and spinners are all involved at some time or other. Some of these are closely associated with particular weeds, particular depths of water, and some occur close inshore. In fact skilled and observant anglers often catch most of their trout within fifteen yards or so of the water's edge. They do it by concealing themselves behind bankside cover. If this is swept away the angler will be visible to the fish, which will move out into mid-water.

Excessive bank clearance therefore results in another disturbance to that 'balance of nature' whose preservation is so vital to the life of the countryside.

CHAPTER 22

Fringe Benefits

I<small>F THE</small> pondside trees need slashers and billhooks, the stream-side growth often needs at most a sickle, and perhaps no more than a pair of secateurs. It is clearance in a minor key. The pity is that it is often undertaken in a spirit of open warfare, as though those rightful denizens of the river bank were deadly enemies. They are nothing of the kind; on the contrary, they are impartial attendants, offering security alike to fish and fisherman.

If anything, they offer more to the angler than to his quarry, for they are things of beauty, and a thing of beauty, as Keats observed, is a joy for ever.

> Its loveliness increases; it will never
> Pass into nothingness; but still will keep
> A bower quiet for us, and a sleep
> Full of sweet dreams, and health, and quiet breathing.

Where an Itchen-side stream makes a sudden bend you come to a bankside clump of purple loosestrife, whose tall spires mingle with the massed mauve flower-heads of hemp agrimony, presenting a spectacle to arrest the most concentrated angler. Each time I go that way in high summer I know the flowers will be there, yet they always startle with the same surprise, the same delight. From the water meadows on the other side they stand out like a landmark.

Much of the banks along this mile and a half of river and side streams are fringed throughout with a fine collection of flowering plants. Among the first to appear is the richly nectared butterbur, later giving way to its huge leaves under which many a lusty trout will take up residence. Then come the purple flowers of comfrey, with here and there white-and-yellow-petalled specimens. There is a pinkish-red loosestrife, and also the unrelated yellow—a plant used by the Romans to protect their horses from flies. There are majestic stands of great hairy willow-herb, tallest of the tribe, meadowsweet and wild mimulus, and—half hidden in herbage—many plants of modest dress. Everywhere there are reeds, sedges and their attendant warblers.

It is a chalk-stream environment where man works with nature, imposing upon her beautiful extravagance only the absolute minimum of interference consistent with the provision of high-class trout fishing. From this pattern, and from similar ones elsewhere, it is clear that streamside vegetation, correctly controlled, is not a snare for fishermen's flies, nor a booby trap into which anglers will sink to the midriff.

There are, on some chalk streams, long stretches of river devoid of flowering plants. Casting is simplicity itself, but what a wealth of colour and interest is missing. I cannot help associating such stretches with anglers who have never learnt to cast from cover, or whose sole aim is catching fish, having no regard for the hues and the hum of riverside life. When a river bank is denied its flowering plants, there is more than a loss to human senses. Nature is her own best buttress, her own best safeguard against collapse. We see it in a thousand ways, from the small stonecrop which, even while its roots are foraging, holds a wall together, to the gigantic beech whose writhing roots above ground bind the soil of a steep bank. So it is with riverside herbage, strengthening bank edges, defeating erosion, and helping the structure to withstand the tunnelling of voles.

Along a bank well bonded by flowering plants you can walk almost to the water's edge, the line of growth being the only barrier. Along one destitute of these, in water-meadow country, there is often a margin of quagmire. This may be of little consequence in casting terms, but in terms of erosion it is of great consequence, for it is weak territory into which the river is ever probing.

Waterside plants are a boon to trout, offering the shelter which all trout seek. True, the fish are hard to get, but that is one of the things that make trout fishing what it is. There was a time when anglers loved challenge, whenever circumstances demanded the cool calculation, the cautious peep through the rushes, the silent withdrawal. They knelt, crawled, perched on their haunches, lay flat on their faces, and would have had a fair go at tying themselves into knots, had they deemed it expedient. It was all part of the craft of stalking, and they knew that nothing aids a trout stalker more than a great clump of plants, or a screen of rushes.

And where would fishing diaries be without their tales of cunning and circumvention, of grand strategy and split-second tactics? Even Skues palls ever so slightly now and again, when the fish come too easily. But catch him at that magical moment when the light is fading, the blue-winged olives are up, and a lovely two-pounder lies tucked under whispering willow wands. There is only one way: a cast from the other bank, and a long, squelching detour through head-high rushes to the little half-forgotten foot plank far downstream. Agonising minutes are plucked from the fleeting twilight. But it is better to have cast and lost than never to have cast at all.

And the plodding, midge-maddened journey leads to just one throw; muff it, and his troutship will vanish from human ken. It is the very stuff of trout fishing, the stuff of dreams for the winter fireside. What do they know of it who know nothing of rushes and willowherb and such? Their fishing is bereft of strategy, their tactics are the mere mechanics of casting.

There was once an angler casting over just such a bright company of plants as bedecks the Itchen stream bend. Among its flowers it seemed to conceal a magnet, so persistently did they collect that poor fellow's fly. At last, in a fury of frustration, he laid about those flaunting guardians of the trout until they were reduced to tatters. In the commotion, the fish fled. Yet a little change of tactics, and the plants would have been saved, and he might have netted his fish. Each time it was the back cast that tangled the fly, either when the angler was false casting, or on those few occasions when his fly actually hit the water, missed the trout, and came to be lifted off. All that was needed was a slightly faster line speed, a slightly higher cast, and an earlier lift off the water, before the fly had gathered slack—elementary points that scarcely occur outside a 'First Steps in Fly Fishing'.

But they are faults which, if not overcome, will inevitably lead to that frame of mind in which waterside plants are thought of as a confounded nuisance, to be shorn away the moment they send out their first questing leaves. That they can present obstacles, nobody would deny. But the surmounting of these, by skill, judgement and, if necessary, by the long detour to the opposite bank, is all part of the fly fisher's game. Banish the plants, and not only do we impoverish the scene but we also drain away the very essence of trout fishing. I do not advocate a raging jungle, but a fringe, controlled where necessary by cutting gaps, topping extreme growth, and by thinning—all done at places where there is obviously no alternative casting spot to an expected or recognised lie.

Plants do not, in any case, fringe every yard of a river, and it is what stands behind, rather than what stands in front, that matters most. So long as the back area is clear, one eye can be on the fish, the other on the plants; and wonderful it is to measure a trout's nose in inches while missing the meadowsweet by centimetres. One of my best trout lay underneath a long arching spray of reed stems. If the fly was to attract, it had to go over that arch. Over it went, to land at the appointed place. The trout took and shot forward. I moved the rod sideways towards the middle of the stream, the line slipped off the arch, the reel sang, and the way was clear. It was not skill, just a bare-faced fluke, but anglers who are denied the chance to try such 'minor tactics' never know how lucky they might be.

So let the reeds bow, let the flowers have their bright day, and we will judge the passage of the fly by just that little more than a hair's breadth, if we are to be fly fishers. We shall recall that most artful dodger who lay secure from the faint-hearted, but fell at length to our bold insinuation, and mighty fellows we shall be.

CHAPTER 23

The Good-Sized Trout

SEATED ONE day, not at the organ, but at the fireside of a fishing inn, I was confronted by the glazed, immortal eye of a mighty trout who, behind his glass-fronted haven, considered me implacably with a frozen mild surmise. The legend on the tablet told his weight, his captor, the date of capture, words that were stamped not only in brass, but in history.

The tale was told many times, and what matter if at each telling the battle lasted a little longer, the fish took a few more yards of line, plunged into one more weedbed? There he was, for all the world to see, the outward and visible manifestation of 6lb of imperial splendour. There was no need to add to that, and no denying it. His taking marked an epoch, beside which the falling of empires was as the flicking of a spent match.

Those were the great days of trout fishing, when fish were of a size natural to trout, and when the odd six-pounder, or even four-pounder, was a warrior who deserved every inch of his showcase, every tankard raised in his honour, every fancy that his conqueror set free to flit about the winter fireside.

All that is changing, and like so many things that change today, it is for the worse. We live in the age of the illusionists, not harmless chaps with top hats and rabbits who evoke amazement in the young, and happy disbelief in the worldly, but exploiters of human credulity.

Now, even the princely trout has been sucked into their maw. Scientists abhor the normal. They must be forever tinkering with genes and gametes and spermatozoa and other God-given and marvellous-sounding things which are none of their business, in their efforts to 'improve', which means to make bigger, grosser and, in the case of fish, uneatable.

This pernicious process has excited the minds of some fishery owners, which is a vast pity, for fishery owners as a breed are balanced men. We are told that trout of less than 4lb are hardly worth taking. One recognises the sense of publicity, but deplores the evident lack of knowledge of the true art of trout fishing, of the patience needed to deceive, the dexterity needed to hook, play and net a fighting two-pounder.

What would the old masters have said of it all? Again and again their diaries tell of good trout, fine trout, splendid trout, all within a size range natural to the fish. Plunket Greene's 'best trout' was 3¾lb. On a 'wonderful day' at Long-parish his bag of 6½ brace weighed 22lb, just over 1½lb average. The writings of Skues are full of one- to three-pounders, with an occasional four-pounder, and an odd one lost here and there that might have gone five pounds. 'But what an evening's sport we have had!' cried Charles Kingsley; 'There are six fish averaging 2lb apiece,' and that, mark you, from a rich southern chalk stream.

I do not believe I am alone in thinking that there are few things in trout fishing quite so dull as being tolerably certain that the fish will be some huge, dispirited thing that might make one bad-tempered lunge, and then will come sullenly in, bowed under a weight of stupefied resignation. Indeed, people have whispered to me, or even proclaimed it, loud and clear, that after this experience they would ten times rather seek out trout of normal size that will give a run for the money, and will prove to be edible.

There is much to be said for tradition, and for following in the wake of better men. There are no greater fly fishers living today than those magicians of the past like Skues and Halford,

Marryat and Greene, and no finer sportsmen. True, they
would have recognised that things change, that in angling, as
in all human activities, the urge to discover and to gather
knowledge is irresistible. It is what makes the world go
round. But knowledge can be wisely used, or it can be abused
to gratify personal vanity and to satisfy popular demands.

One of these is now being met by that unlucky victim
known as the 'Cultivated Fish', a term perfectly in keeping
with an age when pomposity is made to cover multitudes of
mischief. These fish are not 'cultivated'; they are simply
blown up on manufactured food until they can hardly
breathe, and then turned in to be lugged out as 'record fish'.
It is the broiler system brought to its ultimate madness.

What chance have such fish of living any sort of natural
life, of going about their business in the way that nature
intended? And instead of being the quarry of sportsmen, they
are made the prey of pot-hunters.

I am sorry to see the British Record Fish Committee
pandering to this latest fancy, instead of coming out boldly
with 'No cultivated fish will be recognised'.

Let us have done with this nonsense of the huge trout. He
is the greatest delusion yet foisted on to a new race of easily
deluded trout anglers. Any fool can catch him on a sunk cast
strong as a tow-rope, trailing some misbegotten creation on
the end of it. I should know, for I have caught him. He is to
be pitied rather than persecuted. Let the monsters remain
what they once were; great-hearted veterans, covered in
battle honours, who had outwitted all comers until one day
they fell, as, in the end, do all the mighty fall. And though,
like Lucifer, they fell never to hope again, in their embalmed
glory behind the glass they inspired hope and wonderment
in young men with their first fly rods, and set wagging the
tongues of old men in chimney seats, their rods laid aside, and
only memories left.

CHAPTER 24

I Always Call Him 'Sir'

MY FELLOW-ANGLERS called him 'Sam', but to me the diminutive ill-fitted his stately person. Meaty he certainly was, but with equal certainty he was not matey. Though he lived in the age of the common man, he was not of it. By temperament he was of the Age of Elegance. Thus I knew him as Samuel.

He lay within a cave of alder shoots, into which the current was diverted by a weed-bed. It was an extremely well-appointed residence. The green ribbing of the alders filtered sunlight pleasantly, yet provided shade. Wavering watery breezes fanned the leaves, and ripples played about the woodwork. Life within was unhurried, tranquil, and free from all rude intrusions through flank and rear of the cave. The current was just enough to carry food at a gentle pace into Samuel's sanctuary. He never had to go outside that rustic arbour. All he had to do was to cruise up to the opening or drop back to the rear, which he did in accordance with the stages of his meal.

For the hors-d'oeuvre he would lie two feet below the opening, giving himself sufficient time to ponder the tit-bits as they came into view. For the main course he would drop back to the centre, where he would enjoy himself with all the delicate appreciation of the true gourmet; no vulgar lip-smacking, no aggressive gulping, but a gentlemanly savouring of choice fare. When nearly replete, he would retreat to the end of his cave, there to toy with the biscuits and cheese. Then he would sink to the cool depths, slowly, majestically. Had he belched, it would not have been the belch of gluttony, but of thanks.

As befitted the occupant of such a luxurious abode, waited on hand and foot, knowing nothing of how the poor live, Samuel waxed fat, and perhaps a trifle lazy, but he was a trout who had knocked about the world in his youth, and in moments recollected in tranquillity a knowing gleam would light his eye, and you would realise that here was no flabby decadent, but one who was wise in the ways of things that looked like flies but hid sharp little points. He stored this knowledge within his brain, and now it brought him much amusement as I discovered when I set about his downfall.

Assault in any aggressive sense was unthinkable. Such tactics would have been treated with the patrician contempt they deserved; to have slapped any old mess in front of Samuel would have been like slapping down egg and chips in front of a noble lord at four o'clock in the afternoon.

So for a time I did nothing but lie prone amid the bankside grass, with binoculars trained on every movement of my quarry during his dinner, and that was how I came to acquaint myself with his gradual withdrawal from front to rear of his cave as the meal progressed, and with that recollective orb.

It soon became evident that his laziness was more apparent than real, and physical only. Mentally, he was as alert as anyone half his age, and refusals were not due to inertia, but reflected his epicurean tastes. To catch him on the verge of napping was just not on. By the time slumber began to stroke his eyeballs he had back-pedalled to the end of his lair, and to offer him anything there would have been as futile as trying to blow thistledown through a blackberry bush. Likewise, his position for the main course was secure from knavish tricks.

The only stage where Samuel was in the least vulnerable was the hors-d'oeuvre, since his place for this allowed the possibility of floating something down. But it was a very slim chance. Hooking from upstream is ticklish; if Samuel ignored my offering, its retrieve would set his nerves on edge. Would it be better in this event to flip it back quickly, or to pull it out stealthily? In the former case I stood some chance of snagging up in his arbour; in the latter, he would surely spot that odd-looking object drawing away from him.

I had to get upstream, pitch just below the weed bed into that nonchalant but cornucopian little current, and pray to Ate, the divine goddess of mischief. Samuel always began with nymphs. To float a nymph down on a line tight enough to allow for immediate contact at the crucial moment, but never to arrest its progress even for a split-second as it sails into the trout's vision, demands a co-ordination of reflexes denied to most ordinary mortals, but now and again I catch a grayling or two on the downstream cast, so surely if I could hook that lunging creature, there should be hope of hooking the placid Samuel?

One thing was certain I would need a good ten minutes between any failures and time was vital, for he seldom spent more than twenty minutes nymphing, and usually withdrew to his middle station as soon as the duns came down. Would my nymph look more edible dropped into the swirl immediately below the weed, or dropped a foot lower into the glide?

It seemed to me a question of enormous weight, though on later reflection I doubted whether Samuel cared two hoots where it was dropped. Anyway, on the principle of first things first, I pitched it, from behind a clump of willow herb, into the swirl, with cast greased almost to the tip, for I knew that Samuel preferred his nymphs just below the surface.

It was a nice little Partridge and Orange, thinly hackled. It went into Samuel's cave with the loveliest precision, and he, more trusting than I had dared believe possible, sucked it in. But his long experience came to his aid, even after three years of sybaritic living, and as I struck I knew that I had not even lightly connected, for I struck nothing but void.

Thus began a season's effort that took me through every nymph pattern which man's ingenuity had devised. Never more than two casts an evening, never less than ten minutes between each. But Samuel had learned his lesson. He did not take again, and as time went by I could almost hear him snigger, 'Here comes that old fool again'. On other occasions I seemed to see his arbour gently vibrating, and put it down to his shaking sides.

But I must not place him in the past tense, for he is still there, jovial, dignified, fat and happy. Sometimes I think he winks a sardonic eye as I pass. But I do not wink back, for Samuel would not like familiarity from a social inferior. I bow, bid him good evening, and pass on. And I always call him 'Sir'.

CHAPTER 25

In Praise of River Keepers

LET US now praise famous men. Famous not perhaps in the eyes of the world, for the world's vision is today strangely blurred and often sees fame where there is mere notoriety.

There are, of course, notorious river keepers. One, who shall be nameless, will cheerfully threaten to hurl an intruder into the water, a threat that is accompanied by sundry unflattering doubts about the moral legality of the miscreant's appearance in the world and his general status as a citizen. But in this case notoriety is the mask that fame occasionally wears; that keeper's stretch of river is a model of what a trout stream should be, and there is perhaps no man more dedicated to his job among all the keepers in the land.

To Charles Kingsley the keeper was the 'river-god in coat of velveteen, elbow on knee and pipe in mouth, who, rising when he sees us, lifts his wideawake, and halloas back in a roar of comfort to our mystic adjuration——

' "Keeper! Is the fly up?"

' "Mortial strong last night, gentlemen."

'Wherewith he shall lounge up to us, landing-net in hand, and we will wander up-stream and away.'

Keepers no longer wear velveteen and wideawakes, and perhaps are no longer regarded as river-gods. But their response to the 'mystic adjuration' is likely to be more precise, for the modern river keeper knows all about flies and would probably name the exact species that was emerging, or the type of nymph the trout were taking, or the time of day when a particular fly might be expected.

He knows also about stewponds, raising fish and planning

an introduction programme. He is conversant with fish diseases, with water weeds and their populations of trout food and the vital role they play in creating currents, glides and lies. He knows when and why weeds should be cut, and he understands the need to strengthen banks to provide firm walking by means of buried timbers. A skilled angler himself, he delights in the skill of others. He suffers with sympathy the shortcomings of the tyro, whom he is ever ready to help, and with silence those 'experts' who need no help and will never be taught. There is none so deaf as he who will not listen, which has its fortunate aspects, for the 'expert' does not hear the vocal expression of the keeper's hitherto restrained emotions, when these are released in the less restricted atmosphere of the village pub.

A good keeper regards his river not merely as a means of livelihood but as life itself. In summer you will find him plying his trade from dawn to dusk; in winter his attention is no less slack, for there are fish to be fed in the stewponds, weeds to clear from hatches, not to mention the bottles, cans and all the other rubbish hurled into the river by a supposedly civilised populace. There is clearing and burning along with the general maintenance that keeps a fishery going.

Without his devotion to its wellbeing, the trout stream would die. That may sound an exaggeration to those who think only in terms of hill streams, moorland becks and the like, containing wild fish. These are very different from the chalk stream, which in a fairly short time will become weedy, silted and desolate without the skilled work of the keeper. Two world wars proved that, after each of which it was a Herculean task to bring many stretches back to their former condition. The owners and their keepers performed that task.

River keepers are a race apart. Whether the Joneses keep up with them or not is a matter of sublime indifference. They have more important and worthwhile matters to engage their thoughts.

They have found the true freedom, they live the good life. There is an infinity of wisdom in the old saying that the best things in life are free. The best things are not those for which the restless, frustrated and discontented are endlessly hankering and never discovering. Such people do not even know what it is they seek.

The best things lie among the fields and streams and water meadows and on the windy hills. The universe of nature is the universe of blessedness, and blessed indeed is the man who abides therein. That is the habitation of the river keeper. Let us praise him for tending the silver streams, and in praising let us acknowledge him for the wise man that he is.

Epilogue

THE EVENING rise, the last of the season: it is the saddest time in the fly fisher's year. There is a chill in the September air. Long ago, when it was spring, the large dark olives heralded many days of sunshine and trout. Now they are the large dark olives of autumn, and they herald many days of mournful skies and cold rain and colder winds. But winter, too, has its beauties, bony, austere, its hard, magnificent symmetry.

It is not so much the sense of winter hovering somewhere beyond the farthest down that fills the heart with a sudden melancholy; there will be warmth and brightness yet, for a little while, and fortunes will hang from the beeches. It is more the realisation that when we take down the rod and bid farewell to the waterside, another season will belong to the past.

The days of grace and gaiety, of sedges rustling in sunlight, of the sudden plop of a dabchick that we thought was a swirling trout, the humming days, the odorous days when all the flowers were hosts to all the bees, and when wagtails sported and swallows performed miracles of flight—how fugitive they were.

They were the days of wine and roses, and they were not long. But we have honoured them. We have shared their blitheness, drawn freely of the riches they scattered with such prodigal hands. It is in no sense of self-righteousness that we regard ourselves as being among the elect. Rather is it in a sense of wonder at our astounding fortune.

We who have seen the white flowers of crowfoot gleaming beneath cloudless skies, who have fished cool waters under willow trees and marked the shadows fleeting over land and stream, have gathered treasures beyond all mortal reckoning.

Perhaps we shall not gather them again, or perhaps many still lie in store. Whatever our expectations, we have not, if we possess any wisdom, squandered that glorious bounty, large though it was and illimitable in its splendours.

The light fades over the water meadows; the last trout has gone down and mist curls above the stream. We linger on the footbridge and hear the water, dark now and vague, lapping gently at the willow base where a lusty fish, who should have known better, fell to a Pheasant Tail one evening in June. Hallowed spot, hallowed memory!

Suddenly the days collect. In these few minutes when all is retrospect and the next season a world away, the triumphs and disasters, the battles great and small, the moments of good luck and the moments of luck we persuaded ourselves was bad, but which honesty later whispered was a miserable lack of skill, all return to jostle in the mind.

They leave no room for melancholy. Already we are planning our next season; already it seems nearer. We are making good resolutions, and regret at past mistakes and lost chances is tempered by recollections of worthy victories. The mistakes shall not, we bravely affirm, be made again, though we know that different ones will take their place, for in this game of fly fishing we go on learning to the very end.